MONEY AND SALVATION

An Invitation to the Good Way

Money and Salvation

*An Invitation to
the Good Way*

Andrew Geleris

ST VLADIMIR'S SEMINARY PRESS

YONKERS, NEW YORK

2022

Library of Congress Cataloging-in-Publication Data

Names: Geleris, Andrew, author.
Title: Money and salvation : an invitation to the good way / Andrew Geleris.
Description: Yonkers, New York : St Vladimir's Seminary Press, 2022. | Summary:
  "In this book, Andrew Geleris argues provocatively that we do not give money
  to help the poor but to work out our own salvation. This is not the paradigm
  familiar to most of our contemporaries, but, as Geleris argues, it is the vision of
  the Scriptures, the Church Fathers, and the Orthodox Church"—Provided by
  publisher.
Identifiers: LCCN 2021060615 (print) | LCCN 2021060616 (ebook) | ISBN
  9780881417135 (paperback) | ISBN 9780881417142 (kindle edition)
Subjects: LCSH: Christian giving--Orthodox Eastern Church. | Orthodox
  Eastern Church--Doctrines.
Classification: LCC BV772 .G45 2022 (print) | LCC BV772 (ebook) | DDC
  254/.8—dc23/eng/20220202
LC record available at https://lccn.loc.gov/2021060615
LC ebook record available at https://lccn.loc.gov/2021060616

COPYRIGHT © 2022

ST VLADIMIR'S SEMINARY PRESS
575 Scarsdale Road, Yonkers, NY 10707
1-800-204-2665
www.svspress.com

ISBN 978-0-88141-713-5 (paper)
ISBN 978-0-88141-714-2 (electronic)

PRINTED IN THE UNITED STATES OF AMERICA

Acknowledgements

The deeds of many people have inspired this work. Foremost among them are those of Chana Gdud. One particular incident in her life, described in this book, provides a luminous icon of the utterly breathtaking magnitude of God's love for each of us and our neighbors. Her deed was done in almost complete obscurity. I hope this book helps to elevate her name to the place of honor it deserves among those extremely few righteous souls who have completely devoted their lives to becoming truly human. "The righteous will be in everlasting remembrance" (Ps 112.6 NKJV).

The prayers of St Philaret the Merciful have powerfully aided and influenced this book.

An understanding of the power of sacrificial living and giving have been deeply formed in my life through learning about and experiencing the many compassionate deeds performed by Paul and Marilyn Geleris (my parents) as well as their dear friends Dov Gdud, William Gdud, and Moshe and Basia Brauns. Perhaps one day the world will have the privilege of learning more about the lives of these remarkably merciful people.

This book would not have been possible without the encouragement and frequent wise counsel of my wonderful wife, Jeri. She has been and continues to be the most precious treasure of my life.

Paul Gavrilyuk provided extremely helpful advice and a desperately needed spark of life at a pivotal juncture in the development of this project. Metropolitan Joseph and Fr Michael Gillis gave valuable sage advice and encouragement on several occasions.

I am deeply grateful to Fr Joseph Corrigan for forming and leading a community, St Peter the Apostle Orthodox Church in San Dimas, California, in which I was able to witness and practice many of the spiritual principles discussed in this book. Although we certainly were not perfect, that community showed that the Orthodox vision of miraculous parish life is possible even in twenty-first-century America. How I long to once again participate in the life of such a congregation.

Matushka Brenda Seah did an amazing job painstakingly editing this book and frequently establishing remarkable order out of chaos. Beyond her technical achievements, she often exhibited truly exceptional personal patience and grace in the midst of the frequent irritations with which I bedeviled her.

Finally, many thanks to Fr Chad Hatfield, Sarah Werner, and Fr Ignatius Green of St Vladimir's Seminary for their willingness to publish this book. May the mustard seed of their faith bring great spiritual prosperity to many people and parishes. Most of all may it help satisfy God's unfathomably great thirst for relationship with every person he has created.

Table of Contents

Foreword

Since arriving here to serve as a bishop of the Antiochian Archdiocese of North America, I have been consistently perplexed by the wealth we see in the wider society and the scarcity of resources we find in our churches. The strength of the American economic system does not seem to translate into the financial stability of our parishes or their ability to reach out to their communities.

Paradoxically, most of our people come from places of relative poverty in the Near East, where their churches were financially self-sufficient. When our people achieve personal financial success here, the necessity of funding the Church and her ministries is, therefore, not an obvious one. This dilemma has long concerned me, and I found a wonderful conversation partner in Dr Andrew Geleris, a neurologist and faithful member of our parish of St Raphael in Palm Desert, California. After many conversations about the need to teach our people of the God-given command to give generously to the Church and to the needy, Dr Geleris discussed with me his plans for this wonderful book, and I recommended to him the title: *Money and Salvation*.

In seeing the fruit of Dr Geleris' many years of prayerful study of this vital issue, I wholeheartedly endorse this work. Too often, we as hierarchs, clergy, and lay leaders speak to our people about giving to meet the needs of the church or the needs of the poor, and we forget to teach that the true need for each and every one of us is simply to give. God did not recommend that we give only when there is some perceived need or a capital campaign for a project. God commands that we give for our salvation.

One of the most powerful images he offers is that of the whole burnt offering we see in the Old Testament. Dr Geleris points out that in an agricultural society, the people of God were commanded to offer the first fruits of their crops or livestock to be burned completely. This kind of offering would be akin in our capitalist society to piling cash in the altar and burning it. The point was not where the sacrificial gift was to be used but whether the sacrificial gift was given.

I recommend to all parish clergy and lay leaders that they prayerfully read *Money and Salvation* and work to teach and exhort our faithful to give generously as commanded by our Lord—not only for the building up of our churches but for their own salvation. With gratitude to Dr Geleris for this well-written and well-researched work, and prayers that it will be for the good of the holy Church and the salvation of her faithful children, I remain,

Yours in service of Christ,

+JOSEPH
Archbishop of New York and Metropolitan of all North America
Antiochian Orthodox Christian Archdiocese of North America

Introduction

An utterly breathtaking divergence has developed between the joy of giving that God intends his people to experience and the way many Christians view giving as an unpleasant but necessary obligation of church membership. Bishops, priests, and even ministry leaders often dread talking about finances out of a deep concern about how the faithful will receive their words. But as Jesus said concerning another difficult topic, "From the beginning it was not so" (Mt 19.8). The goal of this book is to dissolve any such feelings of concern and ambivalence regarding church financial discussions by bathing them in the purifying waters of biblical and patristic teaching. It is hoped that the result will be that all of us, clergy and laypeople alike, will feel refreshed—indeed, delighted—by recognizing the unfathomably great blessing God hopes to pour out on us through generosity: "Eye has not seen, nor ear heard, nor have entered into the heart of man the things which God has prepared for those who love him" (1 Cor 2.9).

When you start to read this book, please set aside any thought of your bills, investment accounts, or any other immediate financial concerns. Hide your wallet and checkbook in a separate room, far from your presence both physically and mentally. If anything you read here stirs up feelings of guilt or pangs of conscience that tend to cause you to sense an obligation to give to anybody, even your church or the poor, immediately stop. The purpose of this book is not to raise money for the church or the needy poor. It is to lead each of us to a place where giving is a joyful experience primarily motivated by a sense of gratitude for God's goodness to us and a desire to grow in our experience of his love. If you are not presently at such a place, it is perfectly reasonable not to give anything at the present time. Rather, humbly and prayerfully wait until God grants you the understanding that makes such joyful giving possible.

God wants us, not our money. Many of us often become so pre-occupied with the effort we must exert in order to pursue our own personal ascetic journey that we easily forget that God yearns for our salvation and our blessing far more than we do. Fr Josiah Trenham paints a beautiful picture of the immensity of this longing: "No lover, even if he be violently mad, is so inflamed with his loved one as is God in his desire for the salvation of our souls. God wishes to unite with us more than any lover with his beloved."[1]

This astonishingly great desire of God to unite with each of us partly accounts for the immense priority that God assigns to the topic of money throughout the Bible. The four Gospels record Jesus talking far more about finances than any other single topic except the kingdom of God. When considered as a whole, "Scripture is saturated with teaching on possessions. . . . In terms of the number of verses on possessions, this topic is mentioned in Scripture more than any other: three times more than love, seven times more than prayer, and eight times more than belief. About 15 percent of God's word (2,172 verses) deals with possessions."[2]

By contrast, American Orthodox parishes only rarely dis-cuss financial issues. Indeed, many Christians consider money an "unspiritual" subject in comparison to "truly spiritual" topics such as prayer, fasting, love, forgiveness, obedience, and sexual purity. Many priests intentionally avoid financial discussions out of a compas-sionate desire to avoid adding to the economic burdens of their people, especially those who are poor. On those occasions when we do, reluctantly, talk about money, such discussions typically take the form of gentle invitations for parishioners to prayerfully consider giving in behalf of various exceedingly worthy causes such as the yearly parish budget, repairing a leaky roof, providing scholarships

[1]Josiah B. Trenham, *Marriage and Virginity According to St. John Chrysostom* (Pla-tina, CA: St Herman of Alaska Brotherhood, 2013), 152–153.

[2]Wesley K. Wilmer, ed., *A Revolution in Generosity: Transforming Stewards to Be Rich toward God* (Chicago: Moody, 2008), 26–27.

for young people, acquiring a new icon, constructing new facilities, or even helping the poor. While the causes we seek to support are both worthy and spiritually important, these discussions primarily focus on the need to raise money for the purpose of ministry. These financial discussions are, therefore, "ministry-centric."

Jesus viewed the significance of money through the lens of a dramatically different spiritual paradigm. He never saw money as a means to accomplish ministry, even to help the poor. Instead, every financial discussion he ever had single-mindedly focused on the significance of money for the souls of the people with whom he spoke. Thus, his discussions were "soul-centric." They were ultimately intended to lead us to salvation. For example, when Jesus commanded the rich young ruler to give away all his money to the poor, this had nothing to do with helping the poor. He was trying to remove a significant obstacle to this man's ability to inherit eternal life. Similarly, in the story of the sheep and the goats in Matthew 25, Jesus did not teach that people should assist the needy for the sake of alleviating their suffering. He taught that such charitable acts were essential for the salvation of the donors. As we shall see, the apostle Paul also used this same soul-centric paradigm in his fundraising efforts in behalf of the poor in Jerusalem.

The pages that follow primarily address an Orthodox Christian audience. Nonetheless, some of the theological ideas presented may prove spiritually enriching for readers in other Christian traditions and even for those from other religious backgrounds. The questions at the end of each chapter attempt to aid fruitful personal application and stimulate lively parish small group discussions.

All royalties from the sale of this book will go to St Vladimir's Orthodox Theological Seminary. This offering is given in behalf of two specific prayers. The first is that God will use whatever truth appears in this book to transform the hearts of many people and parishes in order to help satisfy God's deep longing for our salvation. The second is that he will raise up many teachers with far more spiritual maturity and theological expertise than this author to effectively proclaim God's message concerning money and salvation.

The subtitle of this book, "The Good Way," uses the word "Good" both as an adjective and as a noun. Part One of this book discusses God's invitation to us to consider various aspects of the adjectival use of this word, and how financial giving enables us to enter the Way of Jesus (see Jn 14.6). Part Two discusses God's invitation to view the word "Good" as a noun. It discusses various non-financial aspects of the Way and includes the story of a woman whose sacrificial giving of her own life epitomizes the spirit of mercy and generosity that leads each of us to salvation.

Questions for reflection

1. Consider all the instances in the Gospels in which Jesus discussed money, either in parables or while teaching. Can you find any instances where he used a ministry-centric rather than a soul-centric financial paradigm?

2. Is the soul-centric financial paradigm of Jesus too impractical to be used by Orthodox parishes, schools, and charities? Why or why not? How do we measure the success of our financial discussions?

3. Why do many Christians consider money an "unspiritual" topic in comparison to such "spiritual" topics as prayer, fasting, faith, obedience, and sexual purity? What makes a topic "spiritual" or "unspiritual"?

4. What do you think of the following statement: "No lover, even if he be violently mad, is so inflamed with his loved one as is God in his desire for the salvation of our souls. God wishes to unite with us more than any lover with his beloved"? How does this affect your desire to pray, fast, and give?

PART ONE

Financial Giving

I

The Contemporary Lack of Attention to Money

Prayer, fasting, and almsgiving are the three pillars of Orthodox Christian spirituality. They constitute the entire subject matter of Jesus' teaching in the middle section of the Sermon on the Mount in Matthew 6. The Church has subsequently made them the preeminent focus of Great Lent. But while many churches teach extensively about prayer and fasting, they typically devote little attention to almsgiving. A major factor contributing to this neglect is that in English "alms" is an antiquated word with a severely constricted meaning. We often think of it as giving a few dollars to a homeless person by the side of the road or to a Lenten parish collection for the poor. This narrow definition dramatically contrasts with the Church's expansive view of prayer and fasting. We often view prayer as encompassing a wide variety of activities such as morning and evening prayers, participating in liturgical services, the Jesus prayer, spiritual reading, and biblical study. We consider fasting as consisting of not only dietary restriction but also resisting a variety of passions such as gossip, envy, and self-indulgence. A similarly expansive view of almsgiving would include not only giving to the poor but every financial decision individuals and parishes make. It would incorporate deep consideration of the spiritual and theological significance of lifestyle choices, tithing, church building programs, fundraising activities, a willingness to take on debt, and financial contentment. It would also encompass many non-financial acts of personal sacrificial love. In adopting this expansive view of almsgiving, this book will adopt as a matter of definition the terms "finances" and "financial" to refer not only to money but to all our material possessions, including things like our food and clothing. This seems to be appropriate because in our capitalistic economic system almost everything we possess or wish to purchase can be measured in monetary terms.

Our disinclination to discuss almsgiving, especially within the expanded definition of this term just presented, does not faithfully reflect the overwhelming scriptural emphasis on this topic. For example, when Jesus discusses all three spiritual pillars in Matthew 6, over half of the chapter concerns financial matters: three verses address fasting, eleven prayer, and twenty finances. His parables specifically address financial issues more than any other single subject. Even parables that do not directly address financial topics, such as the parable of the good Samaritan or that of the prodigal son, often have crucially important financial components. The current liturgical consciousness of the Church has remained faithful to the emphasis of the Gospels on financial issues. Financial themes dominate about fifteen to twenty percent of every year's Sunday Gospel readings. Excluding the fixed Sunday readings taken from the Lenten Triodion and Pentecostarion would increase this percentage substantially.

A variety of historical and pastoral reasons contribute to our contemporary hesitancy to engage in financial discussions. Historically, we have available to us writings from great monastics and desert fathers on many important spiritual topics such as humility, watchfulness, prayer, fasting, obedience, and love. But we have virtually nothing from them regarding a righteous approach to Christian financial management. In the early centuries of the Church many luminaries such as Sts Clement of Alexandria, Basil the Great, Gregory of Nyssa, Gregory Nazianzen, John Chrysostom, Ambrose, and Jerome discussed financial issues with great prophetic power.[1]

---

[1] Justo L. González, *Faith and Wealth: A History of the Early Christian Ideas on the Origin, Significance, and Use of Money* (Eugene, OR: Wipf and Stock, 2002), 173–198.

But since that time relatively few church leaders have provided additional commentary. This has occurred in large part because governmental support of churches, educational institutions, and charitable organizations in the Byzantine Empire and other predominantly Orthodox countries created little urgency regarding financial topics. The great church historian Jaroslav Pelikan once remarked, "Before Constantine, stewardship might have meant giving your life; after Constantine, stewardship consisted of paying your taxes."[2] More recently the Greek and Antiochian Churches under the Turkish Yoke and the Russian and other Eastern European Churches under Soviet domination had to worry far more about simply surviving than teaching about a Christian approach to financial issues. A final historical factor is that the biblical meaning of the word "stewardship" has become significantly distorted in the Church in America today. The position of *oikonomos* (steward, or household manager) that Jesus refers to, for example, in Luke 12.42, has no comparable job description in our culture. It has therefore become extremely difficult for many Christians to understand the fiduciary responsibility that God intends for us to assume in the management of the financial resources he gives us. In contemporary usage the word "stewardship" has become most strongly associated with church solicitations of donations and pledges, especially as part of year-end "stewardship campaigns." Such a notion of stewardship is precisely the opposite of God's soul-centric financial approach. In recent years several people have attempted to restore to our church culture the true biblical meaning of the word "stewardship." Bill Marianes, with his transformative Stewardship Calling programs, and Fr Robert Holet, with his teaching ministry and wonderful book *The First and Finest: Orthodox Christian Stewardship as Sacred Offering*, have both contributed mightily to this worthy cause. Many other Orthodox efforts have also been undertaken toward this end.

---

[2]Jaroslav Pelikan, "Orthodox America," in *Good and Faithful Servant: Stewardship in the Orthodox Church*, ed. Anthony L. Scott (Crestwood, NY: St Vladimir's Seminary Press, 2003), 193.

One of the most consequential ramifications of the aforementioned historical factors is that the Orthodox Church now lacks a practical, accessible, and prophetic "Christian financial paradigm." Lacking such a paradigm, our seminaries are ill-equipped to provide significant theological training to future priests concerning financial issues. This is in spite of the fact that finances are, as has been pointed out, one of the most prominent themes of the Gospels and the entire scriptural corpus. Clergy seminars rarely focus on equipping current priests to teach about money. And the catalogues of Orthodox publishing houses contain relatively few titles concerning a Christian financial paradigm. Our people have, therefore, been left largely bereft of a truly Christian perspective on how to use their money in a godly way. Undoubtedly, many of them don't even know that such a perspective exists.

In addition to historical issues, pastoral considerations also contribute to the neglect of the topic of almsgiving. This is not because of a lack of spiritual care by priests for their flocks. Quite the contrary: it has occurred precisely because they do care so deeply. Viscerally protective love causes them to instinctively recoil from asking for any financial contributions from poorer members of their parishes. In addition, sometimes they are concerned that wealthier parishioners might misperceive financial discussions as constituting covert and spiritually manipulative fundraising efforts. Finally, priests must sometimes be sensitive to the tendency of some family systems to forbid discussions of money. Their cultural backgrounds may conflate financial success with issues related to personal success, shame, and judgment. To their eternal credit, all our priests would much rather raise less money than compromise the spiritual integrity of their ministries with any of these issues.

The lack of an accessible Christian financial paradigm, the absence of theological training, the unavailability of literature, and pastoral concerns have all conspired together to cause many priests to have a profoundly ambivalent relationship with the topic of money. On the one hand, they are acutely aware of the need for adequate financial resources to fund life-giving ministry. They need money simply to support their own wives and children, provide for youth pastors, create high-quality Orthodox schools, and fund compassionate outreaches to the needy poor. On the other hand, money is often a painfully awkward subject to discuss.

Jesus had no such ambivalence. He therefore felt free to discuss financial issues frequently and powerfully. Pastorally, he completely shared the deep concern of our priests for the financial burdens of poor people. But rather than causing him to shy away from financial discussions, it appears that this concern emboldened his advocacy in their behalf. When he talked to rich people about helping the poor, he even had the temerity to teach them that fulfilling this responsibility had eternal consequences. For example, he said this to the wealthy spiritual elite of his day: "When you give a dinner or a supper, do not ask your friends, your brothers, your relatives, nor rich neighbors, lest they also invite you back, and you be repaid. But when you give a feast, invite the poor, the maimed, the lame, the blind. And you will be blessed, because they cannot repay you; for you shall be repaid at the resurrection of the just" (Lk 14.12–14). But Jesus went far beyond mere financial solicitude in behalf of the poor. He often publicly honored the depth of their daily spiritual struggles in a way that he never did for the rich: "Blessed are you poor, for yours is the kingdom of God" (Lk 6.20).

When it came to speaking to the rich about money, Jesus' overwhelming concern for their salvation completely dwarfed any trepidation he may have felt about their misperception of his motives. For example, he boldly told a parable about a very successful farmer whose material wealth was growing at an astonishing rate but who neglected to pay appropriate attention to spiritual matters. The parable concluded with an unambiguously straightforward soul-centric warning: "'Fool! This night your soul will be required of you; then whose will those things be which you have provided?' So is he who lays up treasure for himself, and is not rich toward God" (Lk 12.20–21).

Paul emphatically admonished Timothy to imitate Jesus' soul-centric approach: "Command those who are rich in this present age not to be haughty, nor to trust in uncertain riches but in the living God, who gives us richly all things to enjoy. Let them do good, that they be rich in good works, ready to give, willing to share, storing up for themselves a good foundation for the time to come, that they may lay hold on eternal life" (1 Tim 6.17–19). Paul himself utilized this same soul-centric approach in his own ministry. When he did fundraising among the Corinthians in behalf of the poor in Jerusalem, he framed his entire "ask" in terms of why giving would be spiritually, and perhaps even financially, profitable for the donors and how it would glorify God. "Whoever sows sparingly will also reap sparingly," Paul wrote, "and whoever sows generously will also reap generously. . . . God loves a cheerful giver. . . . God is able to bless you abundantly. . . . your generosity will result in thanksgiving to God" (2 Cor 9.6, 7, 8, 11 NIV). Likewise, when Paul thanked the Philippians for their generous financial support of him, he said that what pleased him the most was not the gift itself, but the benefit they received from giving it: "Not that I seek the gift, but I seek the fruit that abounds to your account" (Phil 4.17).

In the Sermon on the Mount Jesus provided a theological revelation concerning the spiritual premise for his soul-centric financial paradigm. "The lamp of the body is the eye," he said. "If therefore your eye is good, your whole body will be full of light. But if your eye is bad, your whole body will be full of darkness" (Mt 6.22–23). According to patristic theology the eye of the body to which Jesus refers is the nous, the seat of each person's spiritual perception. The nous is that part of the human being which, according to Metropolitan Kallistos Ware, "understands eternal truth about God."[3] The nous is as important to the body and soul of a human being as the sun is to the earth. With adequate sunlight, life on earth flourishes; without it, everything dies. In the same way, growth in the spiritual

---

[3]Kallistos Ware, *The Orthodox Way*, rev. ed. (Crestwood, NY: St Vladimir's Seminary Press, 1995), 48.

life requires a clean nous, while a darkened nous leads to spiritual death.

This concept has become a fundamental precept of Orthodox pastoral theology. It is the basis of our understanding that purification from all kinds of different passions is an essential step in each person's journey toward illumination and deification. Yet what we often fail to notice is that Jesus proclaimed this teaching as an integral part of an intense and extended discussion of money and material possessions. In the verses immediately before this passage, Jesus challenged his disciples to store up heavenly rather than earthly treasures. The verses immediately after consist of a long discourse encouraging them to trust God to provide for all their physical needs. Therefore, while we rightfully consider purification from a variety of different passions to be important, Jesus deemed dealing with financial passions so essential that he himself initially applied this teaching primarily to how we relate to money and possessions.

Both John the Baptist and Jesus prioritized addressing financial issues as being among the first steps required for repentance. Each of them began their public ministries with identical calls for repentance: "Repent, for the kingdom of heaven is at hand" (Mt 3.2, 4.17). Subsequently, they both also immediately defined this repentance in ways that affected finances. In the case of John, three groups of people asked him how they should begin repenting: the people as a whole, tax collectors, and soldiers.

> The people asked [John the Baptist], saying, "What shall we do then [to repent]?" He answered and said to them, "He who has two tunics, let him give to him who has none; and he who has food, let him do likewise." Then tax collectors also came to be baptized, and said to him, "Teacher, what shall we do?" And he said to them, "Collect no more than what is appointed for you." Likewise the soldiers asked him, saying, "And what shall we do?" So he said to them, "Do not intimidate anyone or accuse falsely, and be content with your wages." (Lk 3.10–14)

Similarly, in the verses immediately after Jesus' initial call for repentance, he asked his disciples to make major financial sacrifices for the sake of following him:

> And Jesus, walking by the Sea of Galilee, saw two brothers, Simon called Peter, and Andrew his brother, casting a net into the sea; for they were fishermen. Then he said to them, "Follow me, and I will make you fishers of men." They immediately left their nets and followed him. Going on from there, he saw two other brothers, James the son of Zebedee, and John his brother, in the boat with Zebedee their father, mending their nets. He called them, and immediately they left the boat and their father, and followed him. (Mt 4.18–22)

Peter subsequently described the magnitude of these sacrifices: "See, we have left all and followed you" (Mt 19.27).

The Gospel account of Zacchaeus (Lk 19.1–10) also shows the importance of monetary issues for repentance. Apparently as a result of being deeply moved by his encounter with Jesus, the first step of repentance that Zacchaeus took was financial, the fourfold restoration of illicitly acquired possessions suggested by the law (see Ex 22.1). It is not clear why he subsequently decided to give away half his goods to the poor, but it does not appear to have been motivated by any further need to repent of past wrongdoing. Perhaps he had heard Jesus teach about the importance of cleansing one's heart from material passions. Perhaps he intuitively understood the importance of almsgiving for salvation. Whatever the reason, it should be noted that it was these financial decisions by Zacchaeus that led Jesus to conclude, "Today salvation has come to this house" (Lk 19.9).

St Anthony the Great and many other desert fathers started their journeys toward salvation by giving away most or all of their money. Even today, poverty and renunciation of material possessions remain a fundamental part of most forms of Orthodox monastic life.

Some people may be tempted to believe that the extraordinary sacrifices of the apostles, Zacchaeus, St Anthony, and today's monastics reflect requirements for spiritual elites but not "ordinary" Christians. But Jesus explained why rightly using our money is essential for every person who seeks the kingdom of God: "For where your treasure is, there your heart will be also" (Mt 6.21). Note the sequence of actions that Jesus describes. First we put our treasure in heaven. Then our hearts follow. Most worldly fundraising efforts, including those that occur within the church, reverse this sequence. They begin by appealing to our hearts with emotionally moving presentations that may include videos, slick brochures, or persuasive talks that describe how desperately our donation dollars are needed and how much good they will do. Often such efforts do successfully raise a lot of money. But they have nothing to do with the soul-centric goal of the gospel, which is to help lead the hearts of people toward salvation.

Financial passions exercise enormous spiritual influence in our lives because the size of our bank account often determines many aspects of our lifestyles. It governs the kind of food we eat, the cars we drive, the adequacy of our health insurance, the quality of the schools our children attend, and whether we live in a small, cramped apartment or a large home with majestic views. If one or both parents must work long hours to support the family budget, such an arrangement potentially undermines marriages and reduces the amount of time parents can spend raising their children. Many working-poor parents live from paycheck to paycheck under a financial sword of Damocles: the fear that an unexpected bill for medical expenses or car repairs might cripple their family budget, making them and their children homeless. Many wealthy people also spend considerable time managing and monitoring their investments.

The availability of financial resources also significantly impacts community life. It frequently determines whether parishes can adequately pay their priests and fund their ministries. It affects how successfully Orthodox seminaries, schools, and charities can accomplish their missions, or even whether they can continue to exist at all. These realities frequently cause bishops, priests, and organizational leaders to bear a heavy burden of concern over the financial health of their organizations and the success of fundraising efforts. Anxiety about money even reaches into monasteries. When an abbot was once asked if his monks ever worried about how the monastery was doing financially, he answered with an ironic smile, "No, they don't. But I do."

Intentional church teaching providing godly perspectives on financial management, including spending, saving, and budgeting decisions, would provide tremendous practical and spiritual benefit to our parishioners. Many of them currently have no other option but to rely on the wisdom of relatives, friends, and worldly financial counselors. Unfortunately, the wisdom available from such sources often does not address the important spiritual issues that underlie many financial decisions. The predictable result of the lack of spiritually wise financial counselors is that many of our faithful have accumulated substantial amounts of spiritually debilitating debt. The lack of godly financial wisdom also means that many wealthier people end up spending much of their money on lavish lifestyles without paying adequate attention to cleansing their nous of financial passions (see Mt 6.19–21). It may be valuable to encourage people to buy Dave Ramsey's books and attend his programs. (He is a bestselling author, radio show host, and popular seminar leader who teaches extensively on financial topics from a Christian perspective.) But a much more holistic solution would be for our churches themselves to teach an Orthodox Christian approach to personal and parish finances. Perhaps multiple parishes could work together to supply spiritually wise and financially prudent advisors to accomplish this. It should be emphasized that such advisors would not give investment advice but focus on helping people understand how to deal with issues regarding debt, financial passions, and generosity in a godly way.

Jesus emphasized financial issues so heavily because the pursuit of money and possessions often constitutes the single greatest competitor within human hearts against our willingness to love God with all our heart. In specifically identifying this competitor, Jesus could have chosen anger, lust, unforgiveness, gluttony, or disobedience, but he didn't. He chose money: "You cannot serve God and mammon" (Mt 6.24). Commenting on this subject, Wesley Wilmer wrote, "Scripture consistently reminds us that if Christ is not first in the use of our money, He is not first in our lives. Our use of possessions demonstrates materially our spiritual status."[4]

Questions for reflection

1. How often do you think about money in your daily life? What kinds of things do you think about? To what extent is God a part of these thoughts? If you are a bishop, priest, or ministry leader, how often do you think about the financial situation of your organization?

2. What do you think about the following statement: "While we rightfully consider purification from a variety of different passions to be important, Jesus deemed dealing with financial passions so essential that he himself initially applied this teaching primarily to how we relate to money and possessions"? Why might dealing with financial passions be helpful in dealing with other passions?

3. How do financial concerns affect your prayer life?

4. Jesus often spoke boldly and fearlessly to rich people about how they used their money, not only in the parables mentioned above but in many other parables and teachings as well. Should we follow his example? Why or why not?

[4]Wilmer, *A Revolution in Generosity*, 25.

5. What do you think about the following statement by Wesley Wilmer: "If Christ is not first in the use of our money, He is not first in our lives. Our use of possessions demonstrates materially our spiritual status"? What does it look like from a practical standpoint to say that Christ is first in the use of our money?

6. Is it appropriate for parishes to try to become places that help people learn to address financial issues from a Christian standpoint, including topics such as budgeting, debt, retirement savings, and generosity? Why or why not? If it is appropriate, then what practical steps might we take to help facilitate that sort of learning?

7. Would you be willing to help your parish develop "a practical, accessible, and prophetic 'Christian financial paradigm'"? How could seminaries and clergy seminars help accomplish such a development?

2

Almsgiving and Salvation

The topic of almsgiving occupies a much more prominent place in Orthodox life than many parishioners realize. The *Orthodox Study Bible* most often uses the word "alms" to translate the Greek word *eleēmosynē*. This Greek word occurs eleven times in the New Testament. Eight times the text translates it as "alms" (Lk 11.41, 12.33; Acts 3.2, 3.3, 3.10, 10.2, 10.4, 10.31, 24.17 OSB) and three times as "charitable deed" (Mt 6.2, 6.3; Acts 9.36 OSB).

According to the *Merriam-Webster Dictionary*, the etymology of the word *alms* is as follows: It descends from Middle English *almesse, almes*, from Old English *ælmesse, ælmes*, which derives from from Late Latin *eleemosyna* (alms), which itself derives from Greek *eleēmosynē* (pity, alms), from *eleēmōn* (merciful), from *eleos* (pity).[1] Thus, our English word *alms* derives its fundamental meaning from the Greek word *eleos*, which means "mercy." Oxford professor of theology David Downs summarizes this translation issue: "The Greek word *eleēmosynē*, often translated as 'alms' or 'almsgiving,' can denote monetary or other material contributions to the poor or, more broadly, *eleēmosynē* can refer to attitudes or actions of mercy."[2] A footnote in the Orthodox Study Bible echoes Professor Downs' observations: "Almsgiving can be translated 'merciful giving.'"[3] Therefore, in the English language, a far more accurate and

[1] *Merriam-Webster* on line, s.v. "Alms," accessed February 23, 2021, https://www.merriam-webster.com/dictionary/alms.

[2] David J. Downs, *Alms: Charity, Reward, and Atonement in Early Christianity* (Waco, TX: Baylor University Press, 2016), 7.

[3] *The Orthodox Study Bible*, ed. St. Athanasius Academy of Orthodox Theology (Nashville, TN: Thomas Nelson, 2008), 966, footnote to Wisdom of Sirach 40.24.

faithful rendering of *eleēmosynē* would use the term "mercy giving." And, instead of using the word "alms," it would often be better to use the word "mercy." Henceforth this book will interchangeably use the terms "almsgiving" and "mercy giving," as well as the words "alms" and "mercy."

This interchangeability opens up a stunning vista of the extraordinarily prominent "hidden in plain sight" place that almsgiving actually occupies in Orthodox worship, private prayer, and theology. The Orthodox faithful pray "Lord, have mercy" far more than any other prayer during most of our liturgical services. It should now be clear that we could just as properly render this petition as "Lord, give alms." The faithful also frequently supplicate God to "have mercy," or "give alms," in the Trisagion Hymn, in David's penitential Psalm 50 (Septuagint numbering; Psalm 51 in the Masoretic text), and in their private morning, evening, and precommunion prayers. Indeed, an appeal for God's mercy/alms constitutes the essence of the most frequent prayer on the lips and in the hearts of the vast majority of Orthodox Christians—the Jesus Prayer. It should not surprise us that almsgiving, one of the three long-hallowed spiritual pillars of Orthodoxy, has such a central role in so many vitally important aspects of Orthodox life.

This centrality reflects the fundamental place almsgiving occupies in Orthodox soteriology. One of the most astonishing and unexpected revelations of the gospel is that how God answers our frequent prayers for mercy largely depends on how generously and mercifully we behave toward needy people. Many poor people in the world's most impoverished countries beg for alms out of desperate financial poverty. Faithful Christians who humbly plumb the depths of their souls readily recognize their own need to beg for God's mercy, or alms, for their desperate spiritual poverty. Financially poor beggars hope that generous passersby will give them the money or leftover scraps of food required to sustain their earthly lives. Spiritually poor Christian beggars hope that the righteous Judge of the universe will give them the mercy required to enter eternal life.

God has inextricably intertwined the hopes of both sets of beggars. Two Sundays before the start of Great Lent the Church urges the faithful to soberly consider the Last Judgment. On that fearsome day we will each discover our eternal destiny, whether God will grant us the mercy for which we have so often supplicated him. The Gospel reading on this Sunday of the Last Judgment teaches that the sole criterion that determines how God answers these prayers is whether we ourselves have shown mercy to needy people: "Then the King will say to those on his right hand, 'Come, you blessed of my Father, inherit the kingdom prepared for you from the foundation of the world: for I was hungry and you gave me food; I was thirsty and you gave me drink; I was a stranger and you took me in; I was naked and you clothed me; I was sick and you visited me; I was in prison and you came to me'" (Mt 25.34–36). On another occasion Jesus concisely taught this same truth: "Blessed are the merciful, for they shall obtain mercy" (Mt 5.7). The following statement, often attributed to St John Chrysostom, summarizes God's revelation of the relationship between rich and poor beggars: "The rich exist for the sake of the poor. The poor exist for the salvation of the rich."

Our salvation, therefore, crucially depends on almsgiving. But it does not transactionally save us because it wins us God's favor. It does not impress God with what good people we are. Pharisees think this way. The power of almsgiving for salvation comes from two interrelated effects that it has on us. First, it helps us grow into the likeness of God. Second, it enables us to experience increasingly the magnitude of his love.

The ultimate destiny of every human life is to grow into God's likeness, to become "partakers of the divine nature" (2 Pet 1.4). In his oration *On the Love of the Poor*, St Gregory of Nyssa explained the efficacy of mercy giving for doing this: "Mercy and good deeds are works God loves; they divinize those who practice them and impress them into the likeness of goodness, that they may become the image of the Primordial Being."[4]

[4] Quoted by Susan R. Holman in *The Hungry Are Dying: Beggars and Bishops in Roman Cappadocia* (New York: Oxford University Press, 2001), 164.

Almsgiving allows us to emulate two of the most prominent aspects of God's character: his generosity and his mercy. The famous words of John 3.16 describe the most astounding example of God's profligate generosity. When God the Father wanted to most definitively manifest his infinite love for the world, he gave the most valuable treasure he could possibly offer: his only begotten Son. Paul wrote of the generosity of Jesus, "Though he was rich, yet for your sakes he became poor, that you through his poverty might become rich" (2 Cor 8.9). Not only these deeds but the stars in the sky, delicate and colorful flowers, chirping birds, majestic mountains, beautiful sunsets, and many other aspects of nature show that the creation itself overflows with the awe-inspiring generosity of God.

The Scriptures also repeatedly describe God's heart of mercy. He constantly attends to the welfare of all who suffer, especially the most financially vulnerable among us, such as widows and orphans. A small sampling of these many scriptural references includes Moses' testimony that "he administers justice for the fatherless and the widow" (Deut 10.18). David describes God as "a father of the fatherless, a defender of widows" (Ps 68.5). Isaiah quoted God as commanding his people to "defend the fatherless, plead for the widow" (Is 1.17). Hosea says of God, "In you the fatherless finds mercy" (Hos 14.3). The apostle James said, "Pure and undefiled religion before God and the Father is this: to visit orphans and widows in their trouble" (Jas 1.27). God himself sternly warned those who do not care for the poor, "You shall not afflict any widow or fatherless child. If you afflict them in any way, and they cry at all to me, I will surely hear their cry; and my wrath will become hot, and I will kill you with the sword; your wives shall be widows, and your children fatherless" (Ex 22.22–24).

But by far God's most definitive and categorical statement concerning his priority of merciful care for the poor occurred at the synagogue in Nazareth at the inauguration of Jesus' messianic ministry. Quoting the prophet Isaiah, Jesus proclaimed the mission statement of his Spirit-filled incarnational presence in the world: "The Spirit of the Lord is upon me, because he has anointed me to preach the gospel to the poor; he has sent me to heal the brokenhearted, to proclaim liberty to the captives and recovery of sight to the blind, to set at liberty those who are oppressed; to proclaim the acceptable year of the Lord" (Lk 4.18–19).

Second, almsgiving leads us to salvation by increasing the capacity of our hearts to experience God's love. His love for us is infinite, whether we love him or not. Long before any of us had the slightest inkling of a desire to start repenting, God already manifested this immeasurable love: "But God demonstrates his own love toward us, in that while we were still sinners, Christ died for us" (Rom 5.8). There is nothing more Christ can do to either show us how much he loves us or work in behalf of our salvation than what he has already done. His work "is finished" (Jn 19.30). Almsgiving, therefore, does not change God's heart toward us; it changes our hearts toward him. It does not cause God to love us more; it expands the capacity of our hearts to experience the love that he already has for us. We ourselves have the power to determine to what degree God's freely offered loving presence becomes a reality in our lives or remains foreign to our experience. Our every act of selfless love opens our hearts to a deeper experiential knowledge of God's love. And every act of selfishness makes his entry more difficult.

One can draw an analogy to how this works by considering the way different people experience music. A concert by a world-famous orchestra that plays music by Bach, Mozart, and Tchaikovsky might provide a deeply meaningful experience for many lovers of classical music. However, those who are not devotees of such music might not enjoy it at all. On the other hand, many young people might thoroughly enjoy a concert featuring famous rap musicians or heavy metal rock music that many of their parents and grandparents might find both aesthetically and even acoustically painful. Thus, in both situations, the same music is experienced differently by different people. The same phenomenon may be observed in the completely contrasting levels of interest and enjoyment that different people may experience while watching a sporting event.

The experience of the love of God works in this same differential way within human hearts. Indeed, even heaven and hell are not distinguished by the presence or absence of the love of God but by varying experiences of the exact same love. Vladimir Lossky eloquently describes God's love as engulfing the entire universe, penetrating into its every nook and cranny. "The love of God," wrote Lossky, "will be an intolerable torment for those who have not acquired it within themselves. According to St Isaac the Syrian, 'those who find themselves in Gehenna will be chastised with the scourge of love. . . . It is not right to say that the sinners in hell are deprived of the love of God. But love acts in two different ways, as suffering in the reproved, and as joy in the blessed.'"[5] St Sophrony of Essex learned this same truth from St Silouan the Athonite: "God is love, absolute love embracing every living thing in abundance. God is present in hell, too, as love. . . . Even in hell Divine love will embrace all men, but, while this love is joy and life for them that love God, it is torment for those who hate Him."[6] According to Metropolitan Hilarion (Alfeyev), one of our greatest church fathers, St Maximus the Confessor, viewed this subject in the same way:

> According to Maximus, human history will be accomplished when all without exception unite with God and God will become "everything to every one." For some this unity will mean eternal bliss, while for others it will become the source of suffering and torment, as each will be united with God "according to the quality of his disposition" toward God. In other words, all will be united with God, but each will have his own, subjective, feeling of this unity, according to the measure of the closeness to God he has achieved.[7]

[5] Vladimir Lossky, *The Mystical Theology of the Eastern Church*, trans. members of the Fellowship of St Alban and St Sergius (Crestwood, NY: St Vladimir's Seminary Press, 1976), 234.

[6] Archimandrite Sophrony, *Saint Silouan the Athonite*, trans. Rosemary Edmonds (Crestwood, NY: St Vladimir's Seminary Press, 1999), 115, 148.

[7] Archbishop Hilarion Alfeyev, *Christ the Conqueror of Hell* (Crestwood, NY: St Vladimir's Seminary Press, 2009), 80.

The blessedness of those who love God does not only affect one's eternal destiny but it manifests itself in this life as well: "According to [Dumitru] Stăniloae, divinization is not only an eschatological gift, but it is also something to be achieved during this life, and then continually fulfilled in eternity."[8] In other words, the reality of heaven is at least to some degree available to us as a present experience in this life that subsequently flows seamlessly across the threshold of death into eternal life. As St Porphyrios of Kavsokalyvia wrote, "Paradise begins here and now."[9] Acts of generosity provide one of the most powerful means by which we can actually know God rather than just know about God.

The powerful presence of God's love in the lives of exceptionally generous people often accounts for the otherwise inexplicable joy and peace that they exude. Even nonreligious sociological research studies demonstrate this phenomenon. In the introduction to their fascinating book *The Paradox of Generosity: Giving We Receive, Grasping We Lose,* Christian Smith and Hilary Davidson discuss what they called the "generosity paradox":

> Generosity is paradoxical. Those who give, receive back in turn. By spending ourselves for others' well-being, we enhance our own standing. In letting go of some of what we own, we better secure our own lives. By giving ourselves away, we ourselves move toward flourishing. This is not only a philosophical or religious teaching; it is a sociological fact.
>
> The generosity paradox can also be stated in the negative. By grasping onto what we currently have, we lose out on better goods that we might have gained. In holding onto what we possess, we diminish its long-term value to us. By always protecting ourselves against future uncertainties and misfortunes, we are affected in ways that make us more anxious and vulnerable to

[8]Radu Bordeianu, *Dumitru Stăniloae: An Ecumenical Ecclesiology* (New York: T&T Clark, 2011), 48.

[9]Holy Convent of the Life-giving Spring (Chrysopigi), *Wounded by Love: The Life and Wisdom of Elder Porphyrios* (Limni: Denise Harvey, 2005), 96.

future misfortunes. In short, if we fail to care for others, we do not properly take care of ourselves. It is no coincidence that the word "miser" is etymologically related to the word "miserable."[10]

Elevating the spiritual pillar of almsgiving to its rightful place alongside prayer and fasting does not diminish the value of these other two disciplines: all three work together. The purification available through prayer and fasting permits our almsgiving to have its full effect in acquiring the likeness of God. As Paul said, "And though I bestow all my goods to feed the poor, and though I give my body to be burned, but have not love, it profits me nothing" (1 Cor 13.3). Likewise, almsgiving greatly aids our fasting and prayer. St Cyprian, the third-century bishop of Carthage, wrote, "Our prayers and fasts have less efficacy, if they are not aided by corporal works of mercy . . . our prayers alone are of little avail for obtaining our petitions, if they are not accompanied by an abundance of deeds."[11] In his first homily on 2 Timothy, St John Chrysostom emphasized the importance of almsgiving for effective prayer:

> For this cause the poor stand before the doors [of the church], that no one may enter empty, but each may do alms at his entrance. You enter to implore mercy. First show mercy. . . . Make God your debtor, and then offer your prayers. Lend to him, and then ask a return, and you shall receive it with usury. God wills this, and does not retract. If you ask with alms, he holds himself obliged. If you ask with alms, you lend and receive interest. Yes, I beseech you! It is not for stretching out your hands you shall be heard! Stretch forth your hands, not to heaven, but to the poor. If you stretch forth your hand to the hands of the poor, you have reached the very summit of heaven. For he who sits

---

[10]Christian Smith and Hilary Davidson, *The Paradox of Generosity: Giving We Receive, Grasping We Lose* (New York: Oxford University Press, 2014), 1.

[11]Cyprian of Carthage, *De opere et eleemosynis* [On works and almsgiving]. quoted in Downs, *Alms*, 96 n. 25.

there receives your alms. But if you lift them up without a gift, you gain nothing.[12]

Furthermore, according to St Isaac the Syrian, the proof that prayer and fasting have purified us is an all-consuming desire to give alms. "This will be for you a clear sign of your soul's limpid purity: when after thoroughly examining yourself, you find that you are full of mercy for all mankind." He then goes on to describe the value of this desire in achieving theosis: "When [a desire for mercy for all mankind] is continually present, the image of the heavenly Father will be seen in you."[13]

Some may wonder whether there is a contradiction between the enormous emphasis described here on the importance of almsgiving for salvation and Paul's teaching that salvation is a gift of God not accomplished by works: "For by grace you have been saved through faith, and that not of yourselves; it is the gift of God, not of works, lest anyone should boast" (Eph 2.8–9). They may also wonder if the same contradiction exists between Paul's words and the teaching of St Maximus the Confessor, in Met. Hilarion's commentary discussed above, that it is the quality of each person's "disposition" toward God that determines who experiences the love of God as "eternal bliss" and who experiences it as "suffering and torment."

In considering this issue we must recall that free will is one of the most important characteristics with which God has endowed each of us. Without free will it would be impossible for any of us to love God or other people. We would be soulless automatons. In the verses that immediately follow the apostle John's famous proclamation of God's amazing sacrificial offering of his Son for the sake of our salvation (Jn 3.16), he proceeds to describe the importance of freely determined choices in order to obtain this salvation:

---

[12]John Chrysostom, *Homilies on 2 Timothy* 1 (NPNF[1] 13:479). Minor stylistic changes made to update the language for modern audiences.

[13]Isaac the Syrian, *The Ascetical Homilies of Saint Isaac the Syrian*, trans. Holy Transfiguration Monastery, rev. 2nd ed. (Boston: Holy Transfiguration Monastery, 2011), 552.

For God did not send his Son into the world to condemn the world, but that the world through him might be saved. He who believes in him is not condemned; but he who does not believe is condemned already, because he has not believed in the name of the only begotten Son of God. And this is the condemnation, that the light has come into the world, and men loved darkness rather than light, because their deeds were evil. For everyone practicing evil hates the light and does not come to the light, lest his deeds should be exposed. But he who does the truth comes to the light, that his deeds may be clearly seen, that they have been done in God. (Jn 3.17–21)

Salvation is a mystery beyond human comprehension. As Paul wrote, "Oh, the depth of the riches both of the wisdom and knowledge of God! How unsearchable are his judgments and his ways past finding out!" (Rom 11.33). In the Epistle to the Ephesians, immediately after describing salvation as a gift, Paul himself offers the kernel of a way to resolve this apparent contradiction: "For we are his workmanship, created in Christ Jesus for good works, which God prepared beforehand that we should walk in them" (Eph 2.10). Thus the grace of God helps save us, both by working mystically in our hearts and by faithfully bringing across the path of our daily lives opportunities for good works, such as suffering people to whom we can show love and mercy. Often such people will be the needy poor, but far more frequently they will be those with whom we have close personal relationships: our spouse, other relatives, fellow parishioners, close friends, and coworkers. Diligently seizing these opportunities for good works "which God prepared beforehand that we should walk in them" (Eph 2.10) allows us to grow in the practice of the mercy which then enables us to receive God's mercy at the final judgment. They also make it possible for us to attain the "disposition" of heart described by St Maximus that allows us to experience the "eternal bliss" of God's love. Thus, salvation occurs as a result of the synergy of both the grace of God and efforts made according to our own free will.

Appreciating the momentous importance of generously giving alms in order to achieve salvation and realizing how often we fail at doing this, may occasionally tempt some of us to despondency. Indeed, on one occasion even Jesus' closest disciples faced this temptation. Recognizing their own inability to accomplish salvific sacrificial giving, they cried out to Jesus in despair, "Who then can be saved?" The answer Jesus gave them offers all of us hope and consolation: "With men this is impossible, but with God all things are possible" (Mt 19.26).

Questions for reflection

1. What do you think about the following two statements?

   a. "Almsgiving, therefore, does not change God's heart toward us; it changes our hearts toward him. It does not cause God to love us more; it expands the capacity of our hearts to experience the love that he already has for us."

   b. "Heaven and hell are not distinguished by the presence or absence of the love of God but by varying experiences of the exact same love."

2. What do you think about the statement that the "sole criterion" that determines how God judges us at the final judgment is how merciful we have been to others (see Mt 25.31–46)? Does this conflict with scriptural statements that suggest that salvation is more of a juridical process or that we are saved by faith alone, such as Romans 10.10, Galatians 2.16, Colossians 2.14, 1 John 4.10, etc.? How does the grace of God bridge this apparent conflict?

3. What do you think about the "generosity paradox" discussed by Christian Smith and Hilary Davidson? What kinds of personal experiences of this have you had in your own life or seen in the lives of other people?

4. What should we do in our parishes to elevate almsgiving to its rightful place alongside prayer and fasting as a spiritually valuable discipline?

5. How should we apply St John Chrysostom's comments about the importance of almsgiving in order to make our prayer in church and at home effective?

6. What were the particular circumstances that prompted Jesus' disciples to be tempted to despair of their salvation (see Mt 19.25)? What does Jesus' response mean when he says, "With men this is impossible, but with God all things are possible" (Mt 19.26)? How does this apply to us?

3

Whole Burnt Offerings

A foundation for understanding the relationship between mercy giving and salvation lies in the Old Testament concept of the whole burnt offering. The Scriptures refer to various kinds of offerings, including whole burnt offerings, sin offerings, grain offerings, and tithes. But by far it most commonly mentions the whole burnt offering. The Orthodox Study Bible uses the word "tithe" or "tenth" in the context of giving an offering fifty-four times and the terms "whole burnt offering" or "burnt offering" over 300 times. The first recorded act of God-pleasing worship was Abel's offering. According to St Cyril of Alexandria, God wholly consumed this offering with fire sent from heaven as a sign that it was acceptable, while nothing happened to Cain's offering.[1] This is how Cain knew that Abel's offering pleased God while his own did not. Noah, Abraham, and Job gave whole burnt offerings. The fact that these offerings occurred before the institution of the law strongly suggests an ontological significance of whole burnt offerings that is relevant even in the Church age. After the proclamation of God's Ten Commandments in Exodus 20, the very next commandment, which otherwise might have been called the "eleventh commandment," was to build an altar to receive burnt offerings and various other kinds of offerings. Moses, Samuel, David, Solomon, Elijah, and many others sought God and worshiped him with whole burnt offerings.

---

[1]Cyril of Alexandria, *Glaphyra on the Pentateuch*, vol. 1, *Genesis*, trans. Nicholas P. Lunn, Fathers of the Church 136 (Washington: The Catholic University of America Press, 2018), 68.

But by far the most significant Old Testament occurrence of an attempted whole burnt offering took place on the occasion of Abraham's journey with Isaac to Mount Moriah. Isaac's poignant question as he carried firewood on his back while Abraham walked beside him carrying a torch with fire revealed the entire purpose of this trip. "My father! . . . Look, the fire and the wood, but where is the lamb for a burnt offering?" (Gen 22.7). As the most explicit Old Testament type of the offering of Christ, the Lamb of God, on the cross, this episode clearly shows that the crucifixion was itself a kind of whole burnt offering.

The feature of the whole burnt offering that most jars our contemporary sensibilities is that no one benefited from it. Fire simply consumed it on the altar. The Old Testament economy largely measured wealth by the size of one's flock or landholdings. We measure wealth by the amount of money one has. Therefore, in order to accurately translate the nature of a whole burnt offering from the Old Testament agrarian paradigm into our capitalistic paradigm, we need to imagine the following scenario: One Sunday a parish collects all its offerings in cash, no checks. Just before the end of the Liturgy, the ushers bring the entire collection forward to the front of the church. At the royal doors, the priest then blesses it and offers it up to God. With great reverence and solemnity, he then carefully lays the money out on the altar—and lights it on fire.

But what purpose did such offerings serve in the Old Testament? And what would be the point of such a "holy fire" in one of our parishes today? Watching thousands of dollars burn on a parish altar would scandalize, offend, and even outrage many people because of the utter wastefulness of such an act. Surely something worthwhile could have been done with this money. The priest could have used it for his own needs, if not many poor people in the community. It could have been used to pay down the church mortgage. However, the very wastefulness and extravagance of such an offering is precisely the purpose for giving it. God doesn't need our offerings. He owns the wealth of heaven. Even the largest gifts of our wealthiest benefactors add nothing to his abundance. Rather, they provide us an opportunity to give sacrificially. They are a means by which we can grow into the likeness of God, becoming imitators of his own profligate generosity.

Not all the offerings in the Old Testament were whole burnt offerings. Tithes supported the liturgical ministry of the temple and helped the poor. A variety of other kinds of offerings served various personal and liturgical functions. However, the frequent occurrence of apparently useless whole burnt offerings undoubtedly kept the fundamentally sacred nature of all offerings at the forefront of the consciousness of the people of God in a way that we have perhaps entirely lost. For them, offerings constituted an integral part of worship, an opportunity to tangibly express love and gratitude to God. For us, offerings are often little more than a means to pay parish bills or fund important ministries. Paradoxically, therefore, the practical wastefulness of the Old Testament whole burnt offerings spiritually enriched their donors, while the practical usefulness of our offerings often spiritually impoverishes us. Their donations elevated their minds to mystery and wonder. Our donations tend to drag our minds down to anxieties about spreadsheets.

John 12 records an example of a "whole burnt offering." Six days before the Passover, Mary, the sister of Martha and Lazarus, poured out a pound of extremely expensive perfume on Jesus' feet. One of the disciples who watched this offering was as outraged by its wastefulness as many of us would be watching thousands of dollars burn on a parish altar. Unable to contain his frustration, he said, "Why wasn't this perfume sold for three hundred denarii and given to the poor?" As you know, the disciple who said this was Judas. Unlike Judas, and perhaps unlike many of us, Jesus had no concerns about the wastefulness of Mary's sacrifice. He defended her offering, saying, "Let her alone. . . . For the poor you have with you always, but me you do not have always."

Jesus did not say this because he did not care about helping poor people. Indeed, he undoubtedly cared more about helping the poor than we do. But he saw that this act of worship transformed Mary's heart in a way that was far more valuable to God than even helping many impoverished people. This is a clear example of Jesus' soul-centric emphasis on financial issues.

Acts 20 records details of Paul's final meeting with the Ephesian elders, a group of friends with whom he had developed close personal relationships during the course of the three years he spent ministering to them. After deeply grieving them by saying that they would never see him again, Paul gave a few final words of instruction. Undoubtedly, he tried to distill for these faithful disciples and close friends the most important spiritual wisdom that he could possibly provide, advice that they could use to guide their own lives, teach their children, and pass along to the Church and all its future members. This was Paul's spiritual last will and testament for them. As his supremely consequential final words Paul quoted a teaching of Jesus that is not otherwise recorded in the Gospels: "It is more blessed to give than to receive" (Acts 20.35). His choice of the topic of giving is a stunning surprise. One might have expected Paul to emphasize the overwhelming importance of love, as he did in 1 Corinthians 13, or to mention one of the great theological themes he developed in the Epistle to the Romans or the Epistle to the Ephesians. Yet not only is his choice of the topic of giving startling, but the whole idea that it is more blessed to give than to receive appears to be utterly nonsensical to many in our present culture. The vast majority of people in this world, even in the Church, would much rather receive a huge financial windfall from a great business investment or winning lottery ticket than give away much of their bank account.

But Paul said this because he understood a profound spiritual mystery. The boundless and uncontainable paschal joy that churches powerfully proclaim and experience at every Easter celebration occurs because Jesus' whole burnt offering on the cross created a new cosmic reality, a radically new way of being. This is the divine source of the inexhaustibly joyful proclamation of the paschal troparion:

"Christ is risen from the dead, trampling down death by death, and upon those in the tombs bestowing life." The paradox of this proclamation is that the means of Christ's defeat of death was death itself. As St John Chrysostom's paschal sermon says, "Let no one fear death, for the Savior's death has set us free. . . . [Hell] took a body and, face to face, met God! It took earth and encountered heaven!"[2] The Old Testament whole burnt offerings are therefore a foreshadowing of Christ's defeat of death by death. This revelation of the work of the cross shatters the worldly paradigm that accumulating wealth is either the means to achieve personal success or the measure of its accomplishment. In the new cosmic reality of the kingdom of God, success can only be experienced by sacrificially giving away wealth and power. Because of our understanding of the transformational power of whole burnt offerings, paying parish bills is no longer simply an obligatory responsibility of church membership, nor are needy people simply potential objects of philanthropy. All these needs, and others like them, are God's sovereign provision for the sake of our eternal salvation.

Every Divine Liturgy clearly epitomizes the profound transformation that such giving enables. For the Liturgy to take place, the parish has a God-ordained need for an offering of very "ordinary" bread and wine to be brought to the Proskomedia. This parallels the occasional God-ordained needs that arise in our parishes and in the lives of the needy poor whom we occasionally meet. In the case of the Divine Liturgy, this bread and wine are subsequently returned to us as the most valuable gift any person could possibly receive: the Body and Blood of Christ. This is precisely the paradigm, the model, for what happens to every "ordinary" sacrificial offering we give for the sake of the love of God. This is the transformation Jesus teaches us will occur when he describes how a seed that falls into the ground "wastefully," so to speak, dies and subsequently bears much fruit

[2]John Chrysostom, *Paschal Homily*. In *The Services of Great and Holy Week and Pascha: According to the Use of the Self-Ruled Antiochian Orthodox Christian Archdiocese of North America*, ed. Joseph Rahal, 3rd rev. ed. (Englewood, NJ: Antakya Press, 2012), 746–747.

(see Jn 12.24). It is the transformation that occurs through a life that becomes "obedient to the point of death, even the death of the cross" (Phil 2.8), so that it then achieves the ultimate place of intimacy at God's right hand.

One important thing to note, however, is that because God's love for us is fully incarnational, if we do not bring any bread and wine to the Proskomedia, then there is nothing for God to transform into the Body and Blood of Christ. Similarly, if we do not bring truly sacrificial offerings to the church, or if we do not help the poor, then there is nothing for God to transform into the experience of resurrection life in our hearts and the circumstances of our lives.

Therefore, in proportion to the degree of gratitude we feel for God's goodness to us, let us consider "wastefully" giving to God with the same unfettered "foolishness" that animated Mary's sacrificial gift. If our life is now filled with hardship so that we have little for which to be grateful, simply offering frequent smiles to complete strangers may be a sacrifice that God greatly rewards. If we have much for which to be grateful, we might consider making a substantial contribution to our parish above and beyond our tithe and usual offerings, perhaps asking that it be largely distributed to needy people. If we feel overwhelmed with gratitude for God's many blessings on our life, we might consider anonymously giving cash, completely setting aside any thought of a tax deduction, to one or more needy families, or perhaps even to a financially struggling priest. And if, apart from any degree of gratitude we might feel, we want to most radically embrace the utterly incomprehensible mystery of the transformational resurrection power of the cross and sacrificial offerings, we might, in complete secrecy, make a truly sacrificial whole burnt offering of a substantial amount of cash with a "holy fire."

Questions for reflection

1. How would you feel watching thousands of dollars burn on a parish altar, including some of your dollars? Would burning money in this way violate Jesus' second great commandment that we love our neighbor as ourselves (Mk 12.31) because we could have used this money to help other people? How is this different than how Judas felt when he saw Mary's "wasteful" offering of perfume? Note that Jesus quoted the second great commandment from the Old Testament (see Lev 19.18). Therefore, when God commanded whole burnt offerings in the Old Testament, was he asking people to violate this commandment in Leviticus? Why or why not? Why was Jesus not bothered by Mary's wasteful offering while it would have probably bothered many of us?

2. What do you think about the following statement: "The practical wastefulness of the Old Testament whole burnt offerings spiritually enriched their donors, while the practical usefulness of our offerings often spiritually impoverishes us"? Why do many of us feel so strongly that all our offerings should fulfill a utilitarian purpose? How much of this way of thinking comes out of a mindset of scarcity rather than abundance when it comes to God and his provision for us and our churches (see Mt 6.25–33)?

3. How might your parish implement a paradigm in which people are encouraged to give entirely for the sake of experiencing God's blessing rather than supporting the parish and its ministries? How would you measure the success of such an effort?

4. What do you think about Jesus' teaching, "It is more blessed to give than to receive" (Acts 20.35)? Is it true? Why or why not? What kinds of blessings might Jesus have had in mind in saying this?

5. What are some kinds of "whole burnt offerings" that you might consider giving in the future? Would you be willing to do the experiment to find out how God would reward giving such an offering?

4

Wealth

One day St Anthony inquired of God why it was that some people were rich and others poor: "Lord. . . . Why are some in penury and others affluent? How do the wicked become affluent while the righteous are impoverished?" A voice came to him that said, "[Anthony], pay attention to yourself, for these are the judgments of God and it is not to your advantage for you to learn about them." In other words, who has wealth and who doesn't is a matter of the providence of God.[1]

Books or articles about wealthy people often describe the grueling months, years, and even decades of arduous work that they undertook to achieve their success. Often, they had to overcome enormous obstacles that required heroic degrees of diligence and personal resiliency to surmount. In addition, many of these people had brilliant minds enabling them to create and execute ideas and plans that dramatically changed the world. These stories fill most of us with admiration and respect. But to the degree that they emphasize the great deeds done by such people to become wealthy, they also occasionally may cause some of us to cringe a little bit inside. The reason for this discomfort is that, in addition to hard work, outstanding business acumen, and heroic resiliency, there is another element that may account for much of the success of wealthy people that is almost universally left out of their stories, and which may be

[1]*Give Me a Word: The Alphabetical Sayings of the Desert Fathers*, trans. John Wortley,, Popular Patristics Series 52 (Yonkers, NY: St Vladimir's Seminary Press, 2014), 31–32.

the most important factor of all. It is, as the Lord told St Anthony, a matter of "the judgments of God."

Many physicians frequently encounter patients for whom becoming wealthy would be impossible. They have severe cognitive or physical impairments due to conditions such as Down's syndrome, refractory seizures, severe multiple sclerosis, disabling strokes, traumatic head injuries, spinal cord injuries, or devastating brain infections. Therefore, any temptation a wealthy person might feel to attribute his financial or professional success entirely to his own efforts must be tempered by the reality that one of the most critical prerequisites for becoming wealthy is simply having reasonably good physical health. In addition, to the degree that wealthy people owe any part of their success to intellectual brilliance or being more clever than other people, they should have the humility to recognize that intelligence is an almost entirely inherited genetic trait.

Circumstances of life also often play a large role in determining who becomes wealthy and who does not. Few people now living in North Korea, Bangladesh, Somalia, or the Amazon jungle have the same opportunity to become wealthy that Americans have. Family of origin is also a significant contributing factor in determining or at least facilitating financial success. Children born into families that encourage hard work and educational achievement often have financial opportunities not available to those born to parents who do not push them educationally. In addition, children who experience physical and sexual abuse while growing up often face severe emotional challenges that make becoming wealthy almost impossible.

Warren Buffett has often attributed much of his success to luck—what he calls winning the "ovarian lottery":

> I've had it so good in this world, you know. The odds were fifty-to-one against me being born in the United States in 1930. I won the lottery the day I emerged from the womb by being in the United States instead of in some other country where my chances would have been way different. . . . Society has something to do with your fate and not just your innate qualities. The

people who say, "I did it all myself," and think of themselves as Horatio Alger—believe me, they'd bid more to be in the United States than in Bangladesh. That's the Ovarian Lottery.[2]

In Deuteronomy, Moses emphasized the importance of avoiding the temptation to believe that anyone can become wealthy apart from the providence of God. Acquiring wealth always and only results from the synergistic efforts of both God and human beings, never from the efforts of people alone.

Beware that you do not forget the LORD your God . . . when you have eaten and are satisfied, and have built good houses and lived in them, and when your herds and your flocks multiply, and your silver and gold multiply, and all that you have multiplies, then your heart will become proud and you will forget the LORD your God. . . . Otherwise, you may say in your heart, "My power and the strength of my hand made me this wealth." But you shall remember the LORD your God, for it is he who is giving you power to make wealth. (Deut 8.11–18 NASB1995)

God's providential purpose for helping some people become wealthy is so that they will have the financial resources required to support the Church and help the needy poor. Alan Barnhart is one deeply committed Christian who has lived out these purposes.[3] While a college student majoring in engineering at the University of Tennessee, he thoroughly studied what the Bible says about money and wealth. He came away from this study with a deep concern regarding the many scriptural warnings about the dangers wealth often poses to a person's spiritual journey. For example, in considering Jesus' parable of the seed scattered on the four different kinds of soil, Alan wasn't too worried about the first two soils. He was, however, deeply concerned about the third one. It was a good

---

[2] Alice Schroeder, *The Snowball: Warren Buffett and the Business of Life* (New York: Bantam Books, 2009), 536.

[3] A seventeen-minute-long video of his remarkable story is available from the following source: Generous Giving, *Alan Barnhart–God Owns Our Business*, June 30, 2014, video, 16:58, *https://vimeo.com/99540117/*, accessed September 2, 2021.

soil in which good seed was planted. But this seed never produced the thirty, sixty, or hundredfold fruitfulness of the same good seed planted in the fourth soil. This was because the growth of the seed in the third soil was choked out by "the cares of this world and the deceitfulness of riches" (Mt 13.22). Therefore, when Alan and his brother took over their parents' small family business in Memphis, they did several things to try to achieve the fruitfulness of the fourth soil and avoid the pitfalls that caused the third soil to be unfruitful. One of the most important of these was to establish a financial "finish line," a predetermined maximum level of income on which they would live even if their business prospered. Any profit they earned above this amount they would give away to the kingdom of God. The finish line they chose was three and a half times the poverty level. Their first year they were thrilled that their business even survived. They gave away the $50,000 they earned above their financial finish line. The second year they had $150,000 to give away. For the next twenty-three years the business grew at a rate of twenty-five percent a year. Thus, within a few years they were giving away a million dollars annually. By about 2008, and ever since, they have given away more than a million dollars a month. The business became worth over $250 million. But despite this huge and growing income Alan and his family continue their relatively simple lifestyle, taking an income of three and a half times the poverty level. He has chosen to see growth in his income as an opportunity not to increase his standard of living but instead to increase his standard of giving.

Alan once explained that, in addition to striving to become the fruitful fourth kind of soil, there was another reason he arranged his life in this way. He saw the vocation of having wealth as comparable to that of cooks working in a military kitchen. In order to regularly provide nutritious meals to thousands of troops, cooks require a lot of expensive equipment and regular supplies of vast amounts of meat, dairy products, fruits, and vegetables. However, if instead of using this equipment and these supplies to feed the troops, the cooks kept the best food back for themselves while only feeding the troops rice and beans, the local general would soon become incensed at this behavior. Alan saw a clear analogy between how cooks in the kitchen receive their provisions of food and equipment in order to feed the troops and how Christians with wealth receive their financial provision in order to supply the needs of the kingdom of God. He thought it was entirely wrong for Christians with wealth to spend God's money primarily on themselves.

Like Alan Barnhart, St Basil the Great lived out a godly perspective on wealth. He inherited great riches from his parents that he subsequently gradually gave away in order to help the poor in many innovative and creative ways. He used his considerable entrepreneurial abilities not for the sake of building his own kingdom but for the sake of the kingdom of God. Among the most significant of his achievements was the establishment of the Basiliad, a large complex of buildings that included what could be considered the very first hospital,[4] where physicians, nurses, cooks, and servants provided medical and hospice care for the sick, and where employment and training in trades was provided for the able poor.[5] The complex included businesses that employed the poor, facilities for accommodating travelers, and monasteries. In the latter, in addition to praying, monks actively modeled Christ's compassion for all men not only by serving the poor but also by providing spiritual guidance and visible models of godliness. In his article on the Basiliad, Timothy Miller notes that St Gregory of Nazianzus "compared the Basileias [*sic*] to the Seven Wonders of the ancient world. But whereas the pyramids of Egypt and the Colossus of Rhodes had brought only worldly glory to those who had constructed them, Basil's philanthropic foundation offered generous Christians an opportunity for spiritual blessings."[6]

Since he had been very rich and then used his wealth in a godly way, St Basil had the authority to speak about the topic of wealth

[4]Timothy S. Miller, "Basil's House of Healing," *Christian History Magazine*, no. 101 (2011): 12.
[5]Holman, *The Hungry Are Dying*, 74.
[6]Miller, "Basil's House of Healing," 12.

and generosity not only theoretically but also out of significant practical personal experience. In a sermon he once gave on the story of the rich young ruler, St Basil presented the theological understanding that motivated his remarkable efforts. One of the questions which often arises when this story is discussed is whether Jesus' command to the rich young ruler to give away all his wealth applies to wealthy Christians today. By far the most common interpretation given in our churches is that it does not: this was a command that applied only to the unique circumstances of this particular rich man. According to this view, the key issue for those with wealth who wish to follow Christ is not how much money they have but their ability to possess money in a dispassionate way. Some people also believe that Jesus' command to the rich young ruler to give away everything was not primarily intended to address a financial issue but was intended as an antidote to the overweening pride that prompted the young ruler to believe that he had actually fulfilled all of God's commandments.

St Basil took an entirely different approach to this whole issue. He didn't believe that having a dispassionate attitude toward money or curing pride had anything to do with why Jesus commanded the rich young ruler to dispossess himself of his wealth. Instead, he viewed the possession of wealth within the context of fulfilling God's second great commandment, to love one's neighbor as oneself. Therefore, in his sermon on the story of the rich young ruler, St Basil said, as if speaking to the young man, "You are far from fulfilling the commandment . . . that you have loved your neighbor as yourself. . . . For if what you say is true . . . then how did you come by this abundance of wealth? . . . Those who love their neighbor as themselves possess nothing more than their neighbor; yet surely, you seem to have great possessions! How else can this be, but that you have preferred your own enjoyment to the consolation of the many?" And then comes St Basil's summary statement: "For the more you abound in wealth, the more you lack in love."[7]

[7]Basil the Great, "To the Rich," in *On Social Justice*, trans. C. Paul Shroeder, Popular Patristics Series 38 (Crestwood, NY: St Vladimir's Seminary Press, 2009), 43.

Very few people have the deep spiritual maturity required to resist the temptation to spend riches on a nice lifestyle. Without a doubt, Lazarus, the beggar in the bosom of Abraham from whom the rich man in hell begged a drop of water, had a marked advantage for entering heaven compared to the rich man in the parable. He was spared the many extremely powerful worldly temptations that wealthy people regularly experience to spend their money on beautiful homes and other luxuries rather than becoming "rich toward God" (Lk 12.21). Joy Dawson, a highly respected Protestant missionary, once observed that, in her many years of experience, the hardest people in the world to help find salvation were not Muslims, Hindus, Buddhists, Jews, or even atheists. They were wealthy people. Jesus himself said, "It is easier for a camel to go through the eye of a needle than for a rich man to enter the kingdom of God" (Mt 19.24).

Many Americans, including some of us within the Church, see becoming wealthy enough to have an upscale lifestyle and personal renown as synonymous with "success." Those who feel confident that they have the spiritual maturity to do this and still pursue God with all their hearts can find comfort in the exemplary lives of biblical heroes such as Abraham, Isaac, Jacob, Job, Boaz, David, Barnabas, Cornelius, and Joseph of Arimathea. However, it should be noted that all of these people achieved their sanctity not because of the lifestyles that they acquired with their wealth but because of the extraordinary personal righteousness and generosity that they practiced in using it. The Scriptures also contain many warnings concerning the dangers of wealth and power. The vast majority of wealthy people in the Bible, including those who ruled as kings over the people of God, failed miserably in their efforts to achieve spiritual success.

Jesus warned against the accumulation of worldly wealth because it has no eternal value: "Do not lay up for yourselves treasures on earth, where moth and rust destroy and where thieves break in and steal; but lay up for yourselves treasures in heaven, where neither moth nor rust destroys and where thieves do not break in and steal" (Mt 6.19–20). Pursuing wealth tends to weaken the desire of our hearts for the kingdom of God: "For where your treasure is, there your heart will be also" (Mt 6.21). But perhaps the most direct scriptural teaching concerning the dangers of seeking wealth was given by the apostle Paul: "But those who desire to be rich fall into temptation and a snare, and into many foolish and harmful lusts which drown men in destruction and perdition" (1 Tim 6.9).

An incontrovertible fact that receives astonishingly little attention in American Orthodox church culture is that the overwhelming majority of our saints have been poor. This should not surprise us, because our Lord himself, whose path we are to follow, divested himself of all the wealth of heaven and became poor on our behalf. We can see this same pattern of divestment among the lives of almost all those Orthodox saints who for one reason or another started out with wealth, such as St Melania of Rome, St Anthony the Great, St Basil the Great, and St Philaret the Merciful. Each of them gave away most of their wealth long before they died. Even some members of royalty whom we honor as saints, such as St Elizabeth the New Martyr of the Romanov dynasty, at least partially earned their recognition as saints through sacrificial acts of merciful generosity.

God's purpose in providentially bestowing wealth on any of us is so that we can use this money to support the Church and the needy poor and thereby become "God's fellow workers" (1 Cor 3.9). At death each of us with wealth "shall give account of himself to God" (Rom 14.12) for how successfully we have accomplished this calling. At that time some of us may experience deep shame when it becomes clear not only to God but also to our family, friends, and all other created beings how much of God's money we have diverted to our own personal affluent lifestyles. The value of the possessions that we own at death will most clearly demonstrate whether we have laid up treasures for ourselves on earth or whether we have become "rich toward God" (Lk 12.21).

If, however, we have enough spiritual insight to become aware of the precariousness of our situation as we contemplate this final accounting, there are two enormously valuable uses to which we can put this knowledge. First, we can start actually trying to fulfill God's providential purposes for giving us wealth. Many of us will be thunderstruck at how quickly and abundantly God rewards even the smallest steps we take in this direction. We may even find that the joy and many other blessings that he bestows in return for such actions will lead us into more sacrificial acts of generosity than we ever dreamed ourselves capable of accomplishing.

Second, we can choose to have the courage and integrity to straightforwardly and unflinchingly confront the lack of faith and desire to know God that makes it so difficult for us to even want to achieve the daunting criterion of financial righteousness taught by St Basil: "Those who love their neighbor as themselves possess nothing more than their neighbor."[8] We are all free, of course, to excuse ourselves from considering ourselves subject to such an ideal. We can completely disregard the providential nature of wealth and adopt the belief that we deserve our wealth because we have worked harder and smarter than other people. Or we might offer a host of reasons for why accomplishing St Basil's standard, which he himself incarnated by establishing the Basiliad, is an utterly impractical or unrealistic pursuit. Alternatively, we can take a bold and heroic approach. We can forsake any effort at rationalization and choose to wholeheartedly embrace the bitter truth that our spiritual immaturity makes it too difficult for us to love our neighbors as ourselves according to St Basil's teaching. Paradoxically, such a realization will result in our acquisition of a spiritual "asset" of inestimably greater value than any of our financial "assets": the virtue of humility. St Ephraim the Syrian said of this virtue, "Humility is so powerful that even the all-conquering Lord did not conquer without it."[9] St

[8] Basil the Great, "To the Rich," 43.
[9] Ephrem the Syrian, *Homily on Our Lord* 41. In Ephrem the Syrian, *Selected Prose Works*, ed. Kathleen McVey, trans. Edward G. Mathews, Jr., and Joseph P. Amar, Fathers of the Church 91 (Washington: Catholic University of America Press, 1994), 315.

Isaac the Syrian called humility "the raiment of the Godhead."[10] The revelation of our spiritual weakness that wealth therefore indirectly brings us may then become a powerfully transformative spiritual force in our lives. We can then hope to experience the blessing for such humility that Jesus promised: "He who humbles himself will be exalted" (Mt 23.12).

Questions for reflection

1. What do you think about the teaching of the Lord to St Anthony and of Moses to the people of Israel that clearly suggests that acquiring wealth is a matter of the providence of God?

2. In what ways do financial concerns, "the cares of this world and the deceitfulness of riches" (Mt 13.22), affect the growth of the seed of God's word in you? What do you think of Alan Barnhart's commitment to become the fourth soil by establishing a financial finish line? Would it be worthwhile for other people to do this, such as Christian businessmen, retired people, real estate or financial investors, or young professionals?

3. What do you think about the following statement: "God's providential purpose for helping some people become wealthy is so that they will have the financial resources required to support the Church and help the needy poor"? What do you think about Alan Barnhart's analogy that compares God's providential gift of the ability to create wealth to the role of cooks in a military kitchen?

4. What do you think about St Basil's statement that "those who love their neighbor as themselves possess nothing more than their neighbor"?

[10]Isaac the Syrian, *The Ascetical Homilies*, 534.

5. Jesus stated, "It is easier for a camel to go through the eye of a needle than for a rich man to enter the kingdom of God" (Mt 19.24). Why is this true? Given this truth, why do so many people want to become wealthy? What are some of the difficulties wealthy people face when attempting to enter the kingdom of God that poor people don't face?

6. Is it possible to die possessing great wealth and still become a saint? Why or why not? Can you think of any examples of saints who died rich since the incarnation of Christ?

7. What do you think of the following statement: "Such a realization [of our spiritual immaturity] will result in our acquisition of a spiritual 'asset' of inestimably greater value than any of our financial 'assets': the virtue of humility"? Even if some wealthy people do not believe that they have the faith required to give away the vast majority of their money like Alan Barnhart and Basil the Great did, how would becoming more humble help them personally and also help their parishes?

5

Tithing and Scripture

This discussion of tithing is divided into two sections. The first presents a scriptural understanding of the spiritual significance of the tithe. The second explores various practical considerations concerning tithing and almsgiving.

The Old Testament sequentially reveals three major purposes for the tithe, beginning with its first scriptural mention in Genesis and concluding with the final reference to it in Malachi. First, the tithe offers a vitally important means of expressing gratitude to God. Second, the tithe is a holy offering that we can use to grow in our relationship with him. Finally, tithing offers the opportunity to experience tremendous personal blessing. After the discussion of these three Old Testament views of the tithe, the New Testament teaching on this topic will then be considered.

The first two Old Testament mentions of the tithe present it as an expression of thanksgiving to God. The Greek word for thanksgiving is *eucharistia*, which is the ultimate origin of the English word "Eucharist," a word that is often used to refer to the sacrament of Holy Communion.

The first of these references occurs in Genesis 14, which records the history of King Chedorlaomer's conquest of several kings as well as their subjects and a large amount of possessions. When Abram learned that one of the people captured was his nephew, Lot, he promptly mobilized an army that defeated Chedorlaomer, rescued Lot, and recaptured the large amount of wealth that had been taken along with him. Upon Abram's return home from this battle, "the priest of God Most High," Melchizedek, met Abram and did two things. First, "Melchizedek king of Salem brought out bread and wine" (Gen 14.18). St Cyprian, bishop of Carthage, points out that this foreshadows the Divine Liturgy: "Also in the priest Melchizedek we see prefigured the sacrament of the sacrifice of the Lord . . . that is, bread and wine, to wit, [Jesus'] body and blood."[1] Second, Melchizedek pronounced a divine benediction on Abram: "Blessed be Abram of God Most High, Possessor of heaven and earth; and blessed be God Most High, who has delivered your enemies into your hand" (Gen 18.19–20). Out of deep gratitude for all that God had done for him, Abram "gave [the priest of God, Melchizedek,] a tithe of all" (Gen 14.20).

As an expression of deep appreciation for Abram's generous and successful rescue efforts, the king of Sodom offered to give him the vast quantity of his possessions liberated from Chedorlaomer. Surprisingly, Abram refused, saying, "I have raised my hand to the LORD, God Most High, the Possessor of heaven and earth, that I will take nothing, from a thread to a sandal strap, and that I will not take anything that is yours, lest you should say, 'I have made Abram rich'" (Gen 14.22–23). Abram wanted to definitively express his loyalty to God alone and to acknowledge God as the only source of his wealth.

The second scriptural mention of the tithe occurred at Bethel, where Jacob briefly stopped during his journey to Haran, where he was going in order to find a wife. Here Jacob had the famous dream in which he saw angels ascending and descending on a ladder to heaven. Toward the end of this dream the Lord stood above the ladder and gave great promises to Jacob:

> "I am the LORD God of Abraham your father and the God of Isaac; the land on which you lie I will give to you and your descendants. Also your descendants shall be as the dust of the earth; you shall spread abroad to the west and the east, to the north and the south; and in you and in your seed all the families

[1] Cyprian of Carthage, *Epistles* 62.4 (ANF 5:359).

of the earth shall be blessed". . . . Then Jacob awoke from his sleep and said, "Surely the LORD is in this place, and I did not know it." And he was afraid and said, "How awesome is this place! This is none other than the house of God, and this is the gate of heaven!" (Gen 28.13–14, 16–17)

In response to these promises, "Jacob made a vow, saying, 'If God will be with me, and keep me in this way that I am going, and give me bread to eat and clothing to put on, so that I come back to my father's house in peace, then the LORD shall be my God . . . and of all that you give me I will surely give a tenth to you'" (Gen 28.20–22). Just like Abram, Jacob saw the tithe as a means to express thanksgiving to God.

Expressing gratitude for acts of kindness that other people do toward us is essential for nurturing healthy relationships. Conversely, failing to concretely express gratitude often causes severe relational damage. Many people have occasionally had the unpleasant experience of going out of their way to help another person, whether financially or in some other way, without ever receiving any expression of appreciation in return. Sometimes recipients of such help believe that simply having feelings of gratitude for what has been done makes them grateful people. This is a serious mistake. Unless they offer some tangible expression of thankfulness to the one who has helped them, even a simple thank you note, the unrequited benefactor is likely to conclude that his or her love has been taken for granted. Worse yet, the benefactor may conclude that the recipient considers their love and relationship of only trivial value. Among casual friends or acquaintances such a relational breach may cause relatively little difficulty, although it is unlikely that any future acts of generosity will be forthcoming. In close personal relationships, however, such as between husband and wife, between a parent and an adult child, or in close parish relationships, failing to practically express thanks may severely undermine relationships. At the least, it will lead to a cooling of love. Frequent expressions of mutual gratitude are therefore essential to maintaining relational warmth.

The same is true in our relationship with God. One of the most spiritually damaging things any of us can do to ourselves is failing to regularly and tangibly express our gratitude to God for his enormous goodness to us. Simply having feelings of gratitude does not suffice. Because both Abram and Jacob gave their tithes prior to the institution of the Mosaic law, their offerings had nothing to do with liturgical obedience. And since they occurred before God attached any promise of blessing to the tithe, they also had nothing to do with seeking God's future favor. They were entirely tangible expressions of gratitude. The tithe continues to serve this same function today.

The third time the Old Testament mentions the tithe reveals another of its important characteristics: that it is holy. Almost at the end of the book of Leviticus, Moses wrote, "Now all the tithe of the land, whether of the seed of the land or of the fruit of the tree, is the LORD's. It is holy to the LORD" (Lev 27.30). A couple of verses later he makes an additional reference to tithing animals such as oxen and sheep, which are also considered to be "holy."

God himself is the ultimate Holy One. The angelic heavenly choir constantly worships him by singing "Holy, holy, holy is the LORD of hosts" (Is 6.3). We echo this heavenly worship in our Trisagion Hymn: "Holy God, Holy Mighty, Holy Immortal," and we quote it at the beginning of the Anaphora. At the burning bush, God told Moses, "Do not draw near this place. Take your sandals off your feet, for the place where you stand is holy ground" (Ex 3.5). The feasts of God are called "holy convocations" (Lev 23.37). The Body and Blood of Christ that we commune of are holy.

And the tithe is holy.

The connection between the first biblical mention of the tithe and the bread and wine offered by Melchizedek that foreshadowed the Eucharist is significant in two specific ways. First, the tithe and the Eucharist are both gifts that God first gives us that we only secondarily return to him. Second, both of these gifts produce enormous blessing and spiritual transformation in our lives. The central act of all Christian worship, the Divine Liturgy, epitomizes this connection. Prior to the Liturgy, the people of God bring an offering of ordinary bread and wine to the Proskomedia. The bread and wine are the product of enormous investments of hard work and time by many people. Farmers spend long hours preparing soil and planting grain. After many months of patient waiting, they harvest wheat, which millers then grind into flour and bakers make into bread. In the same way, wine is the product of many years of nurturing and pruning grapevines. Once the grapes are picked, it often takes years for skilled vintners to create fine wine. However, it is crucial to note that the extraordinary efforts of farmers, millers, bakers, winegrowers, and vintners would all be futile and fruitless without God's providential provision of the proper soil nutrients, rainfall, and sunlight required to grow wheat and grapes. Thus, the bread and wine that we ultimately bring to the Proskomedia are actually a synergistic product of both the hard work of human beings and the provision of God. The existence of this synergy is clearly proclaimed during the Liturgy itself in the prayer of the priest at the elevation of the holy Gifts. "Thine own of thine own," the priest prays, "we offer unto thee in behalf of all and for all." Thus, a profound dynamic of mutual reciprocity and generosity animates the entire process of both the giving and the receiving of the Body and Blood of Christ.

This synergy is entirely parallel to what occurs with the tithe. From the income we earn through both our diligent hard work and God's provision to us of the health, jobs, and intellect required to work, we take a "holy" tenth and return it to God. We do so with the same eucharistic gratitude that characterized the tithes of Abram and Jacob. It would, therefore, be entirely appropriate for each of us to offer our tithes to God with the same liturgical prayer used to elevate the bread and wine: "Thine own of thine own we offer unto thee."

Elder Aimilianos of Simonopetra said, "Prayer is our inclusion in the life of God, our *perichoresis* in God."[2] The elder's use of the

[2]Elder Aimilianos of Simonopetra, *The Mystical Marriage: Spiritual Life according to St. Maximos the Confessor*, trans. Archimandrite Maximos Constas (Columbia, MO: Newrome Press, 2018), 7.

word *perichoresis* (Greek *perichōrēsis*) evokes an extremely powerful Trinitarian theological concept. The Greek word *perichōrēsis* is a
composite of two words, *peri*, meaning "around," and *chōreō*, meaning (among many other things) "to permeate" or "to pervade." It is
a concept most fully developed in patristic theology by St John of
Damascus as a way to explain the relationship of the three persons of
the Trinity to one another as they remain one in essence: "*Perichoresis*
or mutual indwelling embraces, then, the uniting of the one *ousia*
with the three *hypostaseis* without confusion, blending, mingling,
composition, change, or division of substance."[3]

If the elder Aimilianos, therefore, feels comfortable saying that
in prayer we can move toward *perichoresis* in God, perhaps we can
dare with equal boldness to say something similar concerning the
tithe. Thus, the holy tithe is far more than a financial transaction. It
is a beautiful act of synergistic divine and human giving and receiving that constitutes a kind of *perichoresis*, making us participants in
a divine dance.

After the mentions of the tithe at the end of Leviticus, the law
of Moses contains many instructions concerning how to give and
use the tithe. However, no mention of tithing to God occurs during
the roughly eight-hundred-year interval from the time of Deuteronomy 26.13 until 2 Chronicles 31, where Hezekiah mentions it three
times as part of his spiritual reformation efforts. Nehemiah subsequently mentions tithing seven times in connection with his efforts
to restore the Second Temple.

The book of Malachi contains the final Old Testament mention
of tithing. Through the words of this prophet, God himself speaks
to his people: "'Bring the whole tithe into the storehouse, that there
may be food in my house. Test me in this,' says the LORD Almighty,
'and see if I will not throw open the floodgates of heaven and pour
out so much blessing that there will not be room enough to store
it'" (Mal 3.10 NIV).

[3]Charles C. Twombly, *Perichoresis and Personhood: God, Christ, and Salvation in
John of Damascus*, Princeton Theological Monograph Series 216 (Eugene, OR: Pick-
wick Publications, 2015), 45.

The "holy" nature of the tithe already suggests that it has the power to bless our lives. The holy blessing of a priest, holy water, and Holy Communion all bring good things into our lives. Unfortunately, the understanding of God's blessing on the holy tithe has been corrupted by some Protestant leaders who teach the so-called "prosperity gospel." This is the heretical idea that if one gives money to God, in return God then makes the donor healthy and financially wealthy. This teaching takes a small number of biblical verses entirely out of context and ignores the clear message of the entirety of Scripture concerning how God views wealth. The "prosperity gospel" has nothing to do with true Christian faith.

In order to understand the issue of God's blessing on tithing, it would be helpful to situate once again this issue within the context of the Divine Liturgy. From our standpoint, we approach the Liturgy in order to worship our infinitely worthy God. But in the midst of our worship, God, whose very nature overflows with abounding generosity, blesses us with the gift of the Holy Mysteries, the greatest blessing any human being can ever receive. In the same way, when we make a thanksgiving offering of the tithe to God, he never lets us walk away empty-handed. That is simply not his nature.

A godly pastor once explained God's blessing on tithing in the following helpful way: "When we bless God with our money, God blesses us with the things that money can't buy." The kinds of things that even billions of dollars can't buy are joy in our hearts, peace in our relationships, depth in prayer, and meaning in our lives. A wonderful story that illustrates this truth concerns a family with several young children that decided to tithe despite being in a somewhat tight situation financially. In order to do this, they had to sacrifice their weekly family dinner out at a restaurant and occasional trips to the movies. Instead they stayed home and played board games and went on occasional outings to the local park for barbecue dinners. After a few months the mother and father realized that spending more time together had significantly enhanced their marriage and created much closer relationships with their children.

Many generations of faithful tithers can testify to their experience of God's blessing and reward for tithing. Few of them become rich, but most find something far more valuable than wealth: personal, financial, and spiritual peace.

We have now come to the end of our sequential journey through the Old Testament mentions of the word "tithe." The New Testament uses the word "tithe" ten times. Seven of these mentions occur within a space of just eight verses at the beginning of Hebrews 7. These verses discuss the superiority of Christ's priesthood to the Levitical priesthood because of Abram's tithe to Melchizedek. They will not be further discussed here.

The only three other New Testament mentions of the word "tithe" occur in the Gospels. In the parable of the publican and the Pharisee, Jesus quotes a Pharisee justifying himself: "I fast twice a week; I give tithes of all that I possess" (Lk 18.12). The other two mentions of the word "tithe" occur in Matthew and Luke. These two almost identical passages record Jesus criticizing the hypocrisy of the Pharisees: "Woe to you scribes and Pharisees, hypocrites! For you pay tithe of mint and anise and cummin, and have neglected the weightier matters of the law: justice and mercy and faith. These you ought to have done, without leaving the others undone" (Mt 23.23; Lk 11.42). Note that Jesus' condemnation of the Pharisees concerned their neglect of "the weightier matters of the law: justice and mercy and faith" but not their tithing. Indeed, he explicitly says that they should not have left the commandment to tithe "undone."

Despite this clear teaching, some people reject the spiritual discipline of tithing because they consider it an Old Testament legalism that no longer applies to Christians. There are indeed some Old Testament commandments which the New Testament abrogates, such as circumcision and various dietary laws, but the tithe is not one of them. Implicit in the criticism of tithing as an Old Testament legalism is a complete misunderstanding of the purpose of all God's commandments. Each of them is a profoundly loving expression of his paternal desire for our wellbeing. Legalism is a concern only for those, such as the Pharisees, who perversely twist God's loving purposes for giving commandments to their own selfish ends by parading their external obedience as an opportunity to justify themselves and build up their own egos. But faithful Christians find obedience to the commandment to tithe a pathway to blessing, never a means of personal justification. When parents firmly command a toddler to avoid touching a hot stove and even discipline him for his disobedience, their motivation is to prevent the child from coming to harm. The child is not justified by his obedience; he escapes burning his hand. Likewise, when parents command their ten-year-old child to say evening prayers and briefly read the Scriptures with them, their purpose is not to needlessly deprive their child of playtime. The child's obedience will help form godly habits that will provide a blessing for the rest of her life. This is how it is with all God's commandments. When obeyed with faith they set us on a path of boundless blessing. Thus, for those who truly understand the goodness of God, tithing is an opportunity, not an obligation.

God emphatically underlined the magnitude of the blessing that he desires to pour out on us through obedience to the commandment to tithe in a way that he does not do with any of the many other commandments in the entirety of the Scriptures. Moses clearly taught, "You shall not put the Lord your God to the test" (Deut 6.16 NASB1995). When the devil tempted Jesus in the wilderness to throw himself down from the highest point of the temple, Jesus based his refusal to comply on this particular teaching of Moses: "You shall not put the Lord your God to the test" (Lk 4.12 NASB1995). Thus, Scripture definitively and unequivocally forbids anyone to test God, with one glaring exception: tithing. Indeed, in the passage from Malachi quoted above God actually emphatically commands us to test him regarding tithing: "'Test me in this,' says the Lord Almighty, 'and see if I will not throw open the floodgates of heaven and pour out so much blessing that there will not be room enough to store it'" (Mal 3.10 NIV). Therefore, failing to test God's promise to reward us for tithing is itself an act of disobedience. It is a sin!

Frequently, one of the biggest obstacles to encouraging people to test God by tithing is the confusion that occurs when parishes ask people to tithe, or give offerings, primarily to support the parish budget instead of for the sake of seeking God's blessing. Giving is always entirely a spiritual issue, not a financial issue. If every member of our parishes tithed, then a byproduct of this most certainly would be more than adequate church funding. Nevertheless, we must always make it clear that the reason we want the faithful to tithe is only for the sake of their own personal relationship with God. Such an approach is entirely parallel to how we treat fasting and prayer. We teach that fasting is a spiritual matter, even though it has many salutary health benefits. Similarly, we teach prayer as an entirely spiritual issue, although much scientific research suggests that prayerful meditation enhances intellectual function and promotes an overall sense of inner peace and well-being.

On those rare occasions when parishes may face an unexpected financial crisis, it is entirely appropriate to ask parishioners to donate to help solve these problems. But even in such situations, requests must be made with a holy sense that the need has arisen as an entirely providential opportunity that God is providing to members of the parish in order to stretch their faith in giving.

Questions for reflection

1. What do you think about the following statement: "One of the most spiritually damaging things any of us can do to ourselves is failing to regularly and tangibly express our gratitude to God for his enormous goodness to us. Simply having feelings of gratitude does not suffice"? What do you think about the tithe as a means to express such gratitude to God?

2. What do you think about the following statement: "The tithe is holy"? How does this affect your willingness to tithe?

3. Do you believe God blesses tithing? Why or why not? If you do not now tithe, why not?

4. What do you think about the following statement: "Failing to test God's promise to reward us for tithing is itself an act of disobedience. It is a sin!"?

6

Practical Aspects of Tithing and Almsgiving

A discussion of the practical application of tithing and generosity should begin by clearly pointing out the ephemeral nature of all earthly wealth. As Paul wrote, "For we brought nothing into this world, and it is certain we can carry nothing out" (1 Tim 6.7). After losing his earthly wealth, Job said, "Naked I came from my mother's womb, and naked shall I return there" (Job 1.21). The following anecdote was told about one of the wealthiest men in history, John D. Rockefeller: "After he died, someone asked his accountant, 'How much money did John D. leave?' His reply was classic: 'He left . . . all of it.'"[1]

At the moment of death everyone's net worth becomes zero. Depending on one's situation in life this may come as either a great tragedy or a great boon. For those who have worked hard over the course of many years in order to achieve significant wealth and social status, the sudden loss of these blessings may be extremely painful. But for those whose lives have been consumed by grinding poverty, unrelenting physical suffering, and social scorn, the moment of death may constitute a joyful moment of blissful release. The Orthodox funeral service plainly describes this great equalization that occurs at death by noting that in the grave "kings and beggars dwell together."

---

[1]Randy Alcorn, *Managing God's Money: A Biblical Guide* (Carol Stream, IL: Tyndale House, 2011), 81.

From the perspective of eternity, therefore, only during the relatively brief interval between birth and death does anyone have any control over money. And even this control is somewhat illusory. When, for example, we purchase a home or a plot of land, we claim that we "own" it. However, the land has already seen many owners come and go over the preceding centuries, and one would expect that many more would claim such "ownership" over the land in the future. Therefore, any claim of land "ownership" requires a preposterous suspension of historical awareness. At best, any one of us may claim temporary possession of the rights to the land. This is also true of all the money in our bank and brokerage accounts.

Georges Florovsky describes how St John Chrysostom spoke clearly about all claims to the ownership of personal property:

> He felt that there was but one owner of all things in the world—God himself, the Maker of all. Strictly speaking, no private property should exist at all. Everything belongs to God. Everything is loaned rather than given by God in trust to man, for God's purposes. Chrysostom would add: Everything is God's except the good deeds of man—it is the only thing that man can own.[2]

One of the most interesting paradoxes of the otherwise complete dispossession imposed by death is that the only material asset any of us continues to have use of after death is the small plot of ground in which we are buried.

During our lives God's only financial promise to us is that we will have adequate amounts of food and clothing. Jesus said, "Therefore do not worry, saying, 'What shall we eat?' or 'What shall we drink?' or 'What shall we wear?' . . . For your heavenly Father knows that you need all these things" (Mt 6.31–32). Paul wrote, "And having food and clothing, with these we shall be content" (1 Tim 6.8). We can describe any resources we have beyond these basic necessities

[2]Georges Florovsky, "St John Chrysostom: The Prophet of Charity," in *Aspects of Church History*, The Collected Works of George Florovsky, vol. 4 (Belmont, MA: Nordland Publishing Co., 1975), 79–87, at 84.

as "excess provision." Wise people will certainly try to save some of their current excess provision to provide for future needs, including retirement. However, the most effective way to secure our future financial needs is to seek first the kingdom of God: "But seek first the kingdom of God and his righteousness, and all these things shall be added to you. Therefore do not worry about tomorrow" (Mt 6.33–34). Our "excess provision" occurs for two reasons. First, God's exceedingly great generosity and his love will lead him to bless us with far more than we need. Second, it provides each of us the means by which we can give alms in order to grow into the likeness of his generosity and so become saved.

The first step in the practice of almsgiving is an offering of ten percent of our income to the general fund of our local parish. Occasionally, people describe any offering made to the church as a tithe. This is incorrect. The English word "tithe" simply translates the Hebrew and Greek words for a tenth, or ten percent. The second step is giving offerings to help needy poor people, educational institutions, missionary organizations, monasteries, and charities. We should regularly pray that God will bring opportunities for almsgiving into our daily lives. Because of the clear scriptural description of the tithe as a liturgical act, as we will discuss below, funds for these additional mercy offerings should come out of finances above and beyond the ten percent offering to the parish. This is the basis of the frequently encountered church phrase asking us to give our "tithes and offerings." First, we give our tithe to the parish. Then we give our offerings to the needy.

Our culture often entices people to make large charitable donations for the sake of enhancing their personal reputation or increasing their influence. Sometimes it opens the door to them to have a position on the board of a prominent Orthodox organization. Indeed, some boards explicitly, and others implicitly, want their members to make contributions to the organization because it enhances their standing with grant-making organizations. Occasionally such motivations also creep into church giving, with benefits such as receiving seat on the parish council or leadership in other church activities being given in exchange for gifts to the parish. It should be emphasized that we have every right to seek as much public recognition for our giving as we want. Doing this does not harm anyone but ourselves because it completely robs us of God's reward for our efforts. As Jesus said, "Take heed that you do not do your charitable deeds before men, to be seen by them. Otherwise you have no reward from your Father in heaven. . . . [make it so] your charitable deed may be in secret; and your Father who sees in secret will himself reward you" (Mt 6.1, 4).

Almsgiving is a vastly underappreciated means of building true wealth. Financial investors often expend enormous effort weighing the potential risks and rewards of various investment opportunities. They seek out the most astute financial advisors and diligently study the financial reports of many different companies. Even after such scrutiny, some investments disappoint. And, as I've already mentioned, profits from even the most successful investments evaporate at death. Almsgiving, however, offers completely secure investment opportunities guaranteed by the "good faith and credit" of God himself. In addition, the thirty, sixty, and even hundredfold returns produced in this life by mercy giving will even accompany us through the grave into eternity.

Therefore, the savviest Christian investors will always allocate substantial portions of their financial resources to almsgiving investments. Many people have commented on the wisdom of this approach. As Randy Alcorn summarized the words of the seventeenth-century archbishop of Canterbury John Tillotson: "He who provides for this life but takes not care for eternity is wise for a moment but a fool forever."[3] The Protestant martyr Jim Elliot lived and gave his life according to the following truth: "He is no fool who gives what he cannot keep to gain that which he cannot lose."[4] Jesus

[3]John Tillotson, quoted by Randy Alcorn in *Money, Possessions, and Eternity* (Carol Stream, IL: Tyndale House, 2003), 107.

[4]Jim Elliot's private journal entry on October 28, 1949. In *The Journals of Jim Elliot*, ed. Elisabeth Elliot (Old Tappan, NJ: Revell, 1978), 174.

put it this way: "Sell what you have and give alms; provide yourselves money bags which do not grow old, a treasure in the heavens that does not fail" (Lk 12.33).

One of the topics that sometimes comes up in discussions of tithing is whether the tithe should be given to the parish or just generally to charity. There are four reasons to believe that the tithe, and perhaps most Christian charitable donations, should be given to and through one's local parish.

First, the definite commandment that people should give a certain amount, ten percent, has a liturgical quality to it. No obvious reason explains why God specifies giving ten percent rather than, for example, seven percent or twelve percent. When the faithful participate in various liturgical services, they pray the words that the Holy Spirit has given them through the Church, not their individual prayers. Similarly, God's prescription of this fixed percentage for offerings has a liturgical quality to it. At times God may bring individual needy people across the path of his people—the hungry, thirsty, naked, strangers, sick, and imprisoned described in Matthew 25. God leaves it entirely to each person's personal discernment of his will regarding how much, and even whether, to give in such situations. But the tithe, the ten percent offering, is liturgically specified.

The clear Old Testament commandment that the people of God should give the ten percent offering to the temple underlines its liturgical nature. The New Testament practice continues this tradition. Acts 4 describes the common practice in the early Church of laying offerings "at the apostles' feet." Bringing one's offering to these leaders to distribute as they saw fit was equivalent to making the offering to the Church itself. Following the time of the apostles, in the early centuries of the Church, people customarily brought offerings to the church before the start of the Liturgy, which deacons would then take back to the altar area for blessing. After the Liturgy the deacons would then distribute these offerings to the needy.

The second reason for giving the ten percent offering to the parish is that it brings far more glory to God if needy recipients receive help from the hands of the Church rather than our hands. Let them express gratitude to God, rather than to us. Let them praise his name, not ours. Indeed, the truth is that any money they might have received from us has been given to us by God anyway. Similarly, it would be better for Orthodox schools or charitable organizations to receive financial help from parishes rather than from us as individuals. The gratitude they feel for God's financial provision will then rightfully be directed to God and his Church, rather than to us as individuals. As we shall see in a later chapter, this will also greatly facilitate our ability to earn an eternal reward from God for our generosity rather than an ephemeral earthly reward from other people.

Third, personal gifts to individuals and Orthodox organizations often create awkward or even unhealthy interpersonal dynamics. Few people, even among priests, have the spiritual and emotional maturity required to receive personal gifts without warped relationships as a result. And such gifts can also easily corrupt the hearts of donors. Personal gifts to charitable organizations can also warp relationships, especially if the gifts are tracked within the organizations by various kinds of donor database computer programs.

The fourth and perhaps most important reason for encouraging charitable giving primarily through one's parish is that the spiritual wisdom required to rightly administer such donations does not necessarily accompany either the gift of wealth or a heart of generosity. And, even if it did, surely the conciliar wisdom of a parish community usually far exceeds the individual wisdom of any one individual. Sometimes truly exceptional discernment is required to know if the financial need of a particular individual or organization is the precise means God might be employing to direct them in his will. God often uses financial difficulties to call a person to a season of deeper prayer and purification, move to a different location, look for a different job, get more schooling, or even go to seminary. God may use financial difficulties to direct charitable organizations to pursue new ventures they had never considered or to restructure their organizations. He may even want them to shut down. We should always be eager to give to the destitute poor without overly scrupulously examining their circumstances. However, when it comes to giving to meet the needs of non-destitute people or organizations, we should consider the possibility that such giving might inadvertently lead them in unhealthy directions and even harm them. Steve Corbett and Brian Fikkert have written an excellent book relevant to this topic, *When Helping Hurts: How to Alleviate Poverty without Hurting the Poor . . . and Yourself.*[5] Conciliar discernment within a parish may be the best way to decrease the risk of such dangers.

If many people started tithing to their local parishes, the amount of money at the disposal of these parishes would dramatically increase. At that point parishes must then adopt the financial priorities that Jesus articulated in his messianic mission statement at Nazareth (Lk 4.16–21). They might choose to establish ministries of compassion in their local communities and become significant financial support-ers of our archdioceses, seminaries, schools, charities, monasteries, and missionary organizations. Instead of engaging in fundraising campaigns and hiring development departments, these latter orga-nizations would concentrate on nurturing relationships with parish priests and their people. Such a collaboration would provide a tre-mendous degree of mutual enrichment and cross-fertilization that would greatly profit both parishes and these organizations.

Occasionally the question arises as to whether one should tithe on one's gross or after-tax income. Since the government taxes peo-ple based on their adjusted gross income, Christians should consider honoring God with at least the same respect that they offer civil authorities. The primary question, of course, is not how little we can get away with in honoring God with our tithes, but how much gratitude we can express to him for his goodness to us.

Another issue that sometimes arises regarding tithing is whether one should tithe while still trying to get out of debt. Obviously, doing so seems counterintuitive. However, many people who have never tithed often severely underestimate the spiritual and financial

[5] Steve Corbett and Brian Fikkert, *When Helping Hurts: How to Alleviate Poverty without Hurting the Poor . . . and Yourself* (Chicago: Moody, 2014).

blessing that tithing produces. Several highly respected and experienced Protestant financial experts, including the late Larry Burkett and Chuck Bentley, CEO of Crown Financial Ministries, who have successfully helped thousands of people escape the clutches of debt, strongly recommend tithing as an aid to accomplishing this. If one cannot give a full tithe, then at least starting on the path toward tithing may be valuable.

Here is what Dave Ramsey says on the subject of tithing while still in debt:

> Is it okay to put giving [to the church] on hold when you're throwing every dime at your debt? You might be surprised at my reply. Are you ready? The answer is, no. Here's why: The Bible never mentions anything about hitting the pause button on tithing. Now, it doesn't say we'll go to hell if we don't tithe, but the tithe is clearly a scriptural command from God. In fact, in Malachi 3:10, God actually promises to bless us if we faithfully tithe.
>
> Here's something else ... Many people have noticed that when they *stop* tithing, their finances seem to get *worse*. Whoa. That's why I would never suggest pausing it to pay down debt. You can probably find other areas to trim if you try. If we can't live off 90% of our income, then we probably can't live off 100% either.
>
> Here's what I recommend: When you make your next monthly budget, pay God *first*. Then use what you have left to pay yourself. Take care of food, shelter, transportation and clothing. Then attack those debts.[6]

It is crucial to teach our children at an early age about God's blessing on tithing. Once a person or family has established a certain lifestyle that may include an expensive mortgage, a large car payment, and long-term investment plans, they may find it difficult to

[6]Dave Ramsey, "Should You Give while Getting Out of Debt?," *Dave Ramsey* (blog), October 15, 2019, *https://www.daveramsey.com/blog/give-while-in-debt/*, accessed September 2, 2021.

have enough money available to tithe, much less to give more than a tithe. Young people who start their working careers budgeting to give at least a tithe will then be able to organize their entire financial lives in a spiritual way. People who have achieved substantial financial success in life will find that God's blessings on tithing are exponentially multiplied to those who choose to give to God even more than a tenth.

The old covenant actually commanded the giving of three tithes. The first supported the ministry of the temple, providing for the needs of the clergy and facilities. The third tithe, given every three years, specifically addressed the needs of the poor. The second tithe, given yearly, has largely escaped our attention. We might call it the "celebration tithe." It is mentioned in Deuteronomy (Deut 14.22–26) and Tobit (Tob 1.6–8). People did not give this tithe to the temple. Rather, it funded the large celebrations that occurred when the people of God gathered for the three major old covenant feasts. In our culture we might think of such a "celebration tithe" as an opportunity to cover hotel and meal expenses for large church gatherings such as parish life conferences or clergy-laity gatherings, or diocesan and national assemblies. The purposes of these gatherings include encouraging the spiritual growth of our people and enabling people from different parishes to get to know one another. They also allow our young people to meet future spouses. Unfortunately, the wonderful potential benefits of these conferences are not available to the large number of our faithful who can't afford the hotel and transportation costs required to attend when these conferences occur at luxury hotels and distant venues. Imagine the joy that it would bring to the heart of God, and these people, if money from a second tithe facilitated the attendance of many of our less affluent members. It might even make it possible for these events to become outreaches to non-Orthodox friends. Perhaps holding such conferences at relatively inexpensive venues would also enable more widespread participation among our people. Undoubtedly, many other potential uses of the "celebration tithe" would help manifest the joy and abundance of life in the kingdom of God in our parishes and dioceses.

Many different personal or spiritual reasons may account for an inability or unwillingness to embrace God's gift of tithing. This does not mean that parishes should avoid teaching on this topic. The weaknesses of some should not deprive the rest of the opportunity of learning about God's blessing on tithing. This is the same way churches handle the spiritual discipline of fasting. We clearly teach God's ideal standards while simultaneously making generous pastoral accommodations available to those unable to achieve these standards for whatever reason. Similarly, spiritual fathers could easily provide accommodations for difficulties regarding tithing whenever necessary. For those unable to tithe immediately, spiritual fathers could help parishioners grow toward the goal of tithing by encouraging them to reprioritize their finances a little at a time. They could ask someone to consider giving one percent the first year, two percent the next year, three percent the following year, and so on, until the goal of tithing is achieved.

Those unable to tithe, for whatever reason, can use their knowledge of this weakness as an opportunity to grow in humility. Thus, those who tithe will experience a blessing. And those unable to tithe will also find a blessing.

Just before the discussion of the last Old Testament mention of the tithe in Malachi above, it was mentioned that a long hiatus occurred in the Scriptures between the last mention of tithing in Deuteronomy and its reappearance in 2 Chronicles when Hezekiah attempted to bring spiritual renewal to the people of God. This eight-hundred-year "famine" of teaching about tithing and generosity is eerily similar to the "famine" of financial teaching in today's Orthodox Church. Note the blessing that came upon the people of God as a result of Hezekiah's faithfully teaching God's commandment to tithe:

Moreover [Hezekiah] commanded the people who dwelt in Jerusalem to contribute support for the priests and the Levites, that they might devote themselves to the Law of the LORD. As soon as the commandment was circulated, the children of Israel brought in abundance the first fruits of grain and wine, oil and honey, and of all the produce of the field; and they brought in abundantly the tithe of everything. And the children of Israel and Judah, who dwelt in the cities of Judah, brought the tithe of oxen and sheep; also the tithe of holy things which were consecrated to the LORD their God they laid in heaps. In the third month they began laying them in heaps, and they finished in the seventh month. And when Hezekiah and the leaders came and saw the heaps, they blessed the LORD and his people Israel. Then Hezekiah questioned the priests and the Levites concerning the heaps. And Azariah the chief priest, from the house of Zadok, answered him and said, "Since the people began to bring the offerings into the house of the LORD, we have had enough to eat and have plenty left, for the LORD has blessed his people; and what is left is this great abundance." (2 Chr 31.4–10)

This blessing that Hezekiah made possible for the people of God in his day is fully available to today's Church as well. All that we need are modern-day leaders like Hezekiah who have the courage and willingness to teach about tithing. We may find that people today are just as eager to embrace this message as the people who heard Hezekiah were. If our leaders do this, we will certainly find that God will bless us just as he did the people of Hezekiah's day: "Since the people began to bring the offerings into the house of the LORD, we have had enough to eat and have plenty left, for the LORD has blessed his people; and what is left is this great abundance" (2 Chr 31.10).

Questions for reflection

1. What do you think about the following two statements? (1) "He who provides for this life but takes not care for eternity is wise for a moment but a fool forever." (2) "He is no fool

who gives what he cannot keep to gain that which he cannot lose." How do we determine the balance between giving now to God for the sake of eternity and saving for future retirement needs? How do lifestyle choices affect this balance?

2. What do you think about the four reasons stated above for why most charitable gifts, even those above and beyond the tithe, should be given through our parish? In particular, what do you think about the fourth reason: "The spiritual wisdom required to rightly administer such donations does not necessarily accompany either the gift of wealth or a heart of generosity"?

3. If your parish had increased funds from people tithing, would it be willing to take up the support that is now provided by individuals to Orthodox seminaries, schools, monasteries, and charitable organizations? What might be the benefits to the parish of doing this?

4. What do you think about the following statement: "When it comes to giving to meet the needs of non-destitute people or organizations, we should consider the possibility that such giving might inadvertently lead them in unhealthy directions and even harm them. . . . Conciliar discernment within a parish may be the best way to decrease the risk of such dangers"?

5. How do you think parishes and dioceses could start implementing the second tithe, the "celebration tithe"? How about using it to pay for parish outings simply for the sake of being together and having fun? What do you think about increasing accessibility to parish life conferences and clergy-laity gatherings, or diocesan and national assemblies?

6. Do you think the wonderful results of Hezekiah's fearless example of financial teaching can be replicated today? Why or why not?

7

Parish Almsgiving

The practical example of one particularly dynamic parish, St Peter the Apostle Antiochian Orthodox Church in San Dimas, California, provides a good starting place for a discussion of parish almsgiving. Six practices used by Fr Joseph Corrigan during his tenure as the pastor there enabled significant spiritual and financial success for the parish. All six of these may not work in other parishes, but some of them may be useful. Various problems that occurred in the life of the parish will not be mentioned, taking the advice of the apostle Paul to the Philippians: "Finally, brethren, whatever things are true, whatever things are noble . . . if there is any virtue and if there is anything praiseworthy—meditate on these things" (Phil 4.8).

The first and foremost practice used by Fr Joseph had nothing directly to do with finances. It was his regular and consistent effort to remind his people of the enormous privilege they had in participating in the life and sacraments of the Orthodox Church. This exhilarating vision inspired many in the parish to pursue personal and corporate holiness with far more intensity than they had ever previously done. Out of this milieu there quite unexpectedly emerged a Christian *koinonia* (fellowship or communion) characterized by deep mutual caring and commitment. In order to share their lives more fully, many people in the parish intentionally bought or rented homes in close proximity to one another in a small lower-middle-class neighborhood of Pomona. The children of the parish especially benefited from this arrangement because their friends were close by and their parents felt comfortable letting them frequently visit one another, knowing that they would be well supervised.

Second, Fr Joseph faithfully imitated the example of Jesus by clearly teaching about God's blessing on tithing and generosity, by using a soul-centric approach. There were times when he taught about giving frequently, and there were times when he did not address this topic for long periods of time. Almost everyone found his teaching refreshing. Seemingly miraculous occurrences of God's financial and spiritual blessings related to generous giving happened frequently, both in the lives of individuals and in the parish as a whole. Fr Joseph's teaching also provided a solid spiritual foundation for the children of the parish to learn about tithing.

Third, all donations were collected in a small box with a slot in the top located at the back of the church. Collection plates or baskets were never passed around. Sometimes newcomers who wished to make a donation had to undertake significant effort—a kind of scavenger hunt—in order to locate this box. Its relative hiddenness made many people feel that their giving had a sacred quality, as if God were the only witness of their offerings. They called the donation box a "Joash chest," according to the model of what King Joash commanded in 2 Chronicles 24 and 2 Kings 12.

Fourth, while Fr Joseph intentionally blinded himself to how much any particular person gave, he explicitly tasked the parish treasurer with roughly tracking the giving patterns of each family. Of course, he fully anticipated that spiritually weaker and newer members of the parish would give relatively little, or not at all. However, if someone who had been faithfully giving over an extended period of time suddenly deviated from their usual pattern, Fr Joseph wanted to know. This was not for the purpose of haranguing anyone to give more. He wanted to know because it might indicate that a family was facing unexpected financial hardship with which the parish could help them. It might also be a warning sign that a family was facing serious spiritual trials with which Fr Joseph could help them.

Fifth, Fr Joseph viewed parish finances as a kind of "report card" from God concerning the faithfulness of his pastoral ministry. If the parish was doing well financially, he interpreted this as a sign of God's pleasure. It was not the only measuring stick he used, but it was an important one. If there was financial difficulty, he humbly embraced the possibility that he was doing something wrong in his personal life or parish ministry.

Sixth, and finally, the parish gave a tithe of all the offerings it received to the archdiocese, according to the pattern of the Old Testament (see Num 18.26; Neh 10.38). This was not done out of any sense of obligation or any requirement to support the work of the archdiocese or its ministries. Rather, it was given joyfully with the eager expectation that God would abundantly bless this offering. And, indeed, he did.

While Fr Joseph's six practices brought great financial and spiritual success to his parish, there is another approach that will bring unfathomably great success to any parish's fundraising efforts. It is to make sure that all members of the parish feel deeply loved by their priest and other parish leaders. The importance of this is exemplified by one of the most amazing fundraising miracles in the history of the people of God. In Exodus 35, Moses asked for contributions to build a tabernacle for God in the wilderness. The resultant exuberant outpouring of donations far exceeded the capacity of those tasked with receiving them. Indeed, the Scriptures explicitly say that those who were receiving the offerings had to go to Moses with a request that the people stop giving so much. They "spoke to Moses, saying, 'The people bring much more than enough for the service of the work which the LORD commanded us to do.'" Moses therefore "gave a commandment" for the people to stop giving (Ex 36.5–6). In order to understand why this fundraising miracle happened, we need to understand the context in which it occurred. Shortly before this outpouring of donations occurred, Exodus 32 describes Moses coming down from Mount Sinai after spending forty days with God, only to find Aaron and the people worshiping a golden calf they had just made. God was so angry at this apostasy that he threatened to destroy the people. But Moses interceded for them in an amazing way. "Please forgive their sin," he said to God, "but if not, then blot me out of the book you have written" (Ex 32.32 NIV). In response to Moses' prayer, God relented and did not destroy the people. Therefore, when Moses asked for donations from the people of God in Exodus 35 for the tabernacle, he did not do so simply as their leader. He asked as one who had very recently offered not only his own life but his eternal destiny in their behalf. Their gratitude expressed itself in overwhelming generosity.

Our parishes already do many things that demonstrate the same kind of sacrificial love for their own people that Moses showed for his. One of the most important additional things we could do is to address the widespread Christian financial illiteracy that prevails among large numbers of our faithful. Christian financial illiteracy does not mean that people don't understand how to pay bills and get auto loans. It means that they lack a spiritual understanding of money.

Some people may question whether the Church should even get involved in teaching about financial matters. Certainly, an important reason to consider doing this is that Jesus devoted more attention to this subject than any other. There is also an important theological reason for doing this. The law of Moses makes it clear that spiritual healing, such as atonement for sin, is accomplished through the use of incarnate physical realities such as animals sacrificed on God's altar. As the law of Moses says, "For the life of the flesh is in the blood, and I have given it to you upon the altar to make atonement for your souls; for it is the blood that makes atonement for the soul" (Lev 17.11). Jesus echoed this truth as he passed around the cup of wine at the Last Supper with the words, "For this is my blood of the new covenant, which is shed for many for the remission of sins" (Mt 26.28). In all seven of the great ecumenical councils, the fathers of the Church resisted all efforts to dilute the theological importance of God's incarnation in Jesus. Today we must resist the similar impulse that tends to divorce the importance of physical realities such as money from spiritual pursuits. Animals were a crucially important part of the agrarian culture of the Old Testament, which is in large part why they served such an important role in the liturgical process of atonement. In today's American capitalistic culture, money has a similar place of importance. Perhaps, therefore, if God were to give the law to Moses today, instead of saying that "the life is in the blood," he might instead say, "the life is in the money."

For people of low and modest income the most immediate issue of Christian financial illiteracy is debt. The use of debt is so deeply ingrained in American culture that commercials advertising the sales of cars, household appliances, electronics, and a host of other items typically quote the cost of a purchase in terms of monthly payments rather than a total purchase price. Even if one pays cash for a car, dealers are required by state law to do a credit check. Less than one hundred years ago, buying on credit—what was called an "install-ment plan"—was considered bad Christian morality. An Associ-ated Press wire service report on the forty-second international convention of the Young Men's Christian Association (YMCA) noted the deplorable state of Christian morals among much of the American youth. Along with various sexual issues, one of the major concerns involved "American advertising which creates desire for things not needed; purchasing on the installment plan."[1] Saving enough money to simply buy cars or other major purchases with-out monthly payments has now become rare in the United States, even among churchgoers. Christian financial experts such as Dave Ramsey and the leaders of a highly respected Protestant organiza-tion called Christian Financial Concepts regularly encourage people to buy cars only with cash, even if this means buying a used car.

While no available statistics document how many of our faithful have ongoing credit card debt and how much debt they have, a single anecdote clearly illustrates the poignancy of this problem in our midst. One of the Orthodox Church's most gifted young leaders has

[1]Associated Press, October 25, 1925.

for many years had a very effective ministry regularly feeding and clothing homeless people in his local community. For several years he has had many thousands of dollars of personal consumer debt on which he pays interest of between eighteen and twenty percent. Not surprisingly, worries over this debt burden often intrude into his prayer life and constitute a frequent source of anxiety. They also limit his ability to expand his ministry. As a result of this debt, his personal financial balance sheet shows a significantly negative net worth. Paradoxically, therefore, most of the homeless people whom he faithfully serves have a significantly better balance sheet than he does: their net worth is only zero.

At its root, debt is a spiritual and not a financial issue. The fundamental principle is that God has promised to provide everything we need (see Mt 6.25–34). A corollary of this principle is the "rule of God's financial provision." This "rule" states that, except for emergency needs, if one doesn't presently have enough money to buy something, it simply is not God's will for one to purchase it, at least at the present time. Buying televisions, nonessential consumer electronics, optional clothing, vacations, and sometimes furniture on credit demonstrates a complete lack of faith in God's promised financial provision. Voluntarily submitting ourselves to this rule often helps us to discover the will of God, not only financially but in many other areas of life as well. For example, if living in a certain location requires spending more on housing than we can afford, then perhaps it is God's will for us to move elsewhere. Maybe another parish has an urgent need for the particular kind of ministry we can offer, or perhaps our own spiritual progress requires that we learn from their priest. Maybe our future spouse worships in that parish.

Given the circumstances of our fallen world, certain kinds of debt may at times become impossible to avoid. This may include borrowing money for educational expenses, buying a house with an adequate down payment, or even purchasing a used car so that we can get to work.

Lack of contentment is the primary root cause that underlies a willingness to take on debt. Paul directly addressed this issue when he said, "I can do all things through Christ who strengthens me" (Phil 4.13). This well-known verse is one of the most frequently misused passages in the New Testament. People often use it to provide encouragement to those experiencing significant adversity in life. While such encouragement may be a good thing, Paul clearly wrote these words with a different meaning in mind. The words that immediately precede this verse make it clear that Paul is talking about money, and specifically financial contentment: "I know what it is to be in need, and I know what it is to have plenty. I have learned the secret of being content in any and every situation, whether well fed or hungry, whether living in plenty or in want" (Phil 4.12 NIV). The reason so many people in our country are in debt is because they have not learned the godly contentment that Paul achieved.

One of the greatest tragedies of a willingness to take on debt has nothing to do with the financial strain it causes. Rather, it is that it often makes it difficult for God to bless us financially. Even from a human standpoint, few potential benefactors want to help someone who intends to buy nonessentials on credit regardless of whether a benefactor helps them. The only net result of any financial help provided in such a situation will be to temporarily decrease the size of the recipients' credit card balance. However, since they have not renounced their willingness to take on unnecessary debt, it is almost certain that their level of debt will increase again at some time in the future. Therefore, until the root problem is fixed, no one, not even God, can help. However, a willingness to have even a small amount of faith in God's provision, faith the size of a mustard seed (see Mt 17.20), will allow God to begin to address our financial difficulties. It may even open the possibility that he, perhaps through the hands of one of his servants, will be able to surprise us with unexpected financial provision. But absent a commitment to avoid debt, such help becomes virtually impossible.

Wealthy people also need to grow in Christian financial literacy. Indeed, their need for this may far exceed that of poorer members of their parish. One of the most neglected verses in the Scriptures is Jesus' stern warning that it is very difficult for rich people to enter the kingdom of God (Mt 19.24). Georges Florovsky wrote that St John Chrysostom viewed wealth as a serious danger to spiritual health: "Prosperity was for him a danger, the worst kind of persecution, worse than an open persecution. Nobody sees dangers. Prosperity breeds carelessness."[2]

Unfortunately, many priests and other leaders frequently ignore this terrible danger, "the worst kind of persecution," that wealthy people face. In our highly materialistic culture, many priests are often simply unaware of this danger. But sometimes spiritual leaders avoid addressing the dangers of wealth for selfish reasons. They fear that offending rich people might dry up a valuable source of donations. Just because some people might be sophisticated in their ability to accumulate and manage enormous amounts of worldly wealth does not mean that they have the spiritual wisdom required to use it in a godly way, even for the sake of their own salvation.

Considering the importance of Christian financial literacy even—or especially—for wealthy people, priests should not feel in the least intimidated or fearful at the prospect of having financial discussions with them. Having a priest approach a wealthy person for a discussion about money may initially seem unusual. Church leaders typically only talk to wealthy people in order to solicit donations or seek advice concerning church financial management. But the discussions proposed here would have nothing to do with such issues. They would be entirely soul-centric dialogues discussing the providential nature of the gift of wealth and its purpose of supporting the Church and the needy poor.

The opportunity to have such conversations may be a gift to wealthy people that is far more valuable than most priests can possibly imagine. Having wealth can be a wonderful gift, but it can

[2]Georges Florovsky, "St John Chrysostom: The Prophet of Charity," in *Aspects of Church History*, 80.

sometimes also be a lonely burden. Wealthy people often face a barrage of well-meaning people who want their money and are willing to profess deep bonds of personal friendship in order to obtain it. Even some Orthodox organizations may occasionally "target" them for fundraising efforts. At times they may even find it enjoyable to be "wined and dined" by powerful people and to have occasional access to special "insider" VIP privileges. Such fawning attention, however, sometimes makes it difficult for wealthy people to distinguish their true selves from what they can accomplish with their money. This is one of the ways wealth warps the integrity of our spiritual pursuit. Ultimately, in our deepest moments of profound reflection in the presence of God, what all of us want are friends who love us for who we really are, not for what we can do in their behalf. This is the invaluable gift the priest can offer those with wealth.

Some parishioners will decline this opportunity for conversation. They may feel uncomfortable about discussing the topic of money, or they may lack adequate trust in the wisdom or spiritual maturity of their priest. They may have had previous bad experiences in talking with spiritual leaders about financial subjects. But even in these situations, wealthy people should be encouraged to seek out a spiritual leader whom they do trust in order to have such conversations. Whether we recognize it or not, nothing in the life of a Christian is an entirely private matter. Adam's sin not only compromised his own personal relationship with God, but it also had consequences for every other person in the human race. In the same way, each of our own "private" acts of righteousness or sin, especially those involving money, breathe either life or death into the lives of our brothers and sisters in Christ.

If our spiritual leaders deeply love both our poor and wealthy people by helping to cure their financial illiteracy, then all our people will inevitably experience far more blessing in their lives than they ever previously considered possible. This blessing will become a visible manifestation to our own people and to those around us of the reality that "Christ is in our midst." Out of gratitude for these blessings, and in order to obtain more, many people will inevitably give so exuberantly to their parishes that many priests may one day, like Moses, have to "command" them to stop giving.

Questions for reflection

1. Consider one at a time each of Fr Joseph Corrigan's six practices. Would any of them be worth implementing in your parish?

2. What do you think about the "the rule of God's financial provision," which states, "Except for emergency needs, if one doesn't presently have enough money to buy something, it simply is not God's will for one to purchase it, at least at the present time"? How does Paul's statement, "I can do all things through Christ who strengthens me" (Phil 4.13), apply to this situation?

3. How do you now use, spend, and save money differently than you would if you were not a Christian?

4. What does financial contentment look like in your life? Do you ever feel pride, sadness, or envy as a result of comparing your own financial or lifestyle circumstances to those of other people you know?

5. How has God used your financial circumstances to direct the course of your life?

6. What do you think about the following statement: "Prosperity was for [Chrysostom] a danger, the worst kind of persecution, worse than an open persecution. Nobody sees dangers. Prosperity breeds carelessness"? Why is prosperity so dangerous spiritually? Why do so many people in our churches want to become wealthy anyway?

8

Fundraising

Orthodox parishes and institutions need money in order to function. Stated succinctly: "No money, no mission." The chronic underfunding that plagues many of our parishes and organizations is not primarily a financial problem. It is a spiritual problem. It has not resulted from the poverty of our people. Indeed, Orthodox Christians in this country now control vast amounts of wealth. If most of our faithful gave generously to God, even if they just tithed, their offerings would cover all our financial needs many times over. Rather, the root of our fundraising difficulties is the spiritual illness of covetousness. This sin is rampant in American culture and has, sadly, also deeply insinuated itself into the hearts of many Christians. Increasingly creative and more sophisticated fundraising approaches will never cure this illness. Over time they may even become less effective financially. We need to do two things to solve all our fundraising problems. The first is to clearly teach God's great blessings on tithing, almsgiving, and sacrificial generosity that have been discussed in previous chapters. The second is to help our faithful understand and resist the sin of covetousness. That will be the focus of this chapter.

Any mention of the sin of covetousness may initially seem startling, even offensive, to some of us. In our church culture, covetousness is often considered a "victimless sin" that affects only the spiritual life of the covetous person. The Scriptures, however, suggest that covetousness may have devastating consequences that extend far beyond the confines of our own personal lives. Adam and Eve coveted an apple with disastrous consequences for all of humanity: "Through one man [i.e., Adam] sin entered the world, and death through sin" (Rom 5.12). David coveted Bathsheba, which brought enormous problems on his whole family. As God told David through Nathan, "Now therefore, the sword shall never depart from your house, because you have despised me, and have taken the wife of Uriah the Hittite to be your wife" (2 Sam 12.10). Judas coveted thirty pieces of silver, for which he betrayed the Son of God. Because of this deed Jesus said of him, "It would have been good for that man if he had not been born" (Mt 26.24). Likewise, if we fail to resist covetousness, we risk not only missing out on God's blessing in our lives but bringing on our families and others much unnecessary suffering.

Unfortunately, although this is a crucial topic, the only times many of our churches even discuss it occur during Holy Week, when we contrast the greed of Judas with the generosity of the "sinful woman." In their recent wonderful book about money, John Cortines and Gregory Baumer, both Harvard MBAs, present a helpful definition of covetousness: "Coveting isn't necessarily the desire to steal or take something from someone else. . . . Coveting, at its core, is simply the belief that if I had more, I'd be happy."[1] Fundamentally, it means seeking happiness through the acquisition of possessions rather than a relationship with God. Our culture often labels this way of thinking materialism. The Bible calls it idolatry.

Finding oneself in bed with a woman who is not one's wife makes it easy to recognize the sin of adultery. But covetousness is a far more subtle sin to identify. Most of us easily remember the many times in our lives when we have generously supported various needy individuals and charitable causes. We are, however, often completely oblivious to situations in which God wanted us to give to a particular need but we didn't because our minds were blinded or our hearts were hardened by covetousness. Many of us, therefore,

---

[1]John Cortines and Gregory Baumer, *True Riches: What Jesus Really Said about Money and Your Heart* (Nashville, TN: Nelson Books, 2019), 34.

have a highly inflated estimation of our generosity and virtually no awareness of our greed.

A few years ago, the Assembly of Canonical Orthodox Bishops of the United States of America commissioned Alexei Krindatch to study American Orthodox giving patterns. He found that the average level of Orthodox giving to parishes is three percent.[2] Stunningly, he also found that on a percentage basis, which is how God measures giving, wealthier Orthodox Christians give substantially less than their poorer brethren: "A 'typical' (median) household earning between $30,000 and $49,999 gives 3.75% of its income to the parish, whereas households in [the] $90,000–$109,999 income category give only 2.5%."[3]

Compare these findings to the data cited by Ken Stern in his 2013 article "Why the Rich Don't Give to Charity":

> One of the most surprising, and perhaps confounding, facts of charity in America is that the people who can least afford to give are the ones who donate the greatest percentage of their income. In 2011, the wealthiest Americans—those with earnings in the top 20 percent—contributed on average 1.3 percent of their income to charity. By comparison, Americans at the base of the income pyramid—those in the bottom 20 percent—donated 3.2 percent of their income.[4]

Thus, the levels of charitable giving among Orthodox Christians are only slightly greater than that of Americans as a whole. This suggests that our church is doing a very poor job in teaching about almsgiving, one of the most vitally important spiritual disciplines God has given us.

---

[2] Alexei Krindatch, *Exploring Orthodox Generosity: Giving in US Orthodox Parishes,* September 10, 2015, p. 30, *https://www.assemblyofbishops.org/assets/files/docs/research/OrthodoxGenerosity.pdf,* accessed September 2, 2021.

[3] Ibid.

[4] Ken Stern, "Why the Rich Don't Give to Charity," *The Atlantic,* April 2013, *https://www.theatlantic.com/magazine/archive/2013/04/why-the-rich-dont-give/309254/,* accessed September 2, 2021.

However, we should avoid mistakenly concluding from this data that Orthodox Christians are unwilling to be generous. Such an inference would be unfair, even insulting. Simply learning about the value of resisting covetousness and about God's great desire to bless us through tithing and almsgiving would undoubtedly lead many of our people to joyously give far more abundantly than they now do. But they need to be taught.

The Scriptures repeatedly warn us of the dangers of covetousness. The apostle Paul twice unequivocally equates covetousness with idolatry. To the Ephesians he wrote, "For this you know, that no . . . covetous man, who is an idolater, has any inheritance in the kingdom of Christ and God" (Eph 5.5). The letter to the Colossians says, "Therefore put to death your members which are on the earth: fornication, uncleanness, passion, evil desire, and covetousness, which is idolatry" (Col 3.5). Covetous idolatry is such a significant sin that God makes it an important element in three of the Ten Commandments: the first, the second, and the tenth. By contrast, apart from their connection with covetousness, the sins of adultery, murder, stealing, and lying each appear only once.

The Tenth Commandment explicitly forbids this sin: "You shall not covet" (Ex 20.17 NASB). The First Commandment says, "You shall have no other gods before me" (Ex 20.3 NASB). The second says, "You shall not make for yourself an idol" (Ex 20.4 NASB). When many of us hear "other gods" and "idol," we tend to associate these words with the statues that museums display in their collections of religious artifacts of primitive peoples. Because we don't worship such wooden or clay figures, we quickly dismiss the relevance of these commandments to our lives. This facile rejection blinds us to the ability to recognize that our idols are just as real as theirs, although they take different forms and have different names. The Bible mentions the names of idols such as Baal, Marduk, Dagon, Molech, Milcom, and Ashtoreth. The latter two are idols that King Solomon worshiped (1 Kg 11.5). Americans worship idols with names such as Fame, Wealth, Beauty, and Social Status. Some people in churches worship the idol of being recognized by others for their Spiritual Maturity. We often worship our idols with far more devotion than primitive peoples did their little statues. Their idols remained at family or community altars. We carry our idols around in our hearts. They worshiped their idols only at set times of prayer. We worship our idols all day long as the guides for how we invest and spend our time, energy, and money.

Materialistic covetousness has woven its way so intrinsically into the fabric of our culture that even in church we often have difficulty discerning its presence. For whatever reason, we are highly attuned to sexual sin, and so we often discuss issues such as the dangers of pornography and promiscuity. But we almost never discuss the serious perils of covetousness. Alan Barnhart provides a great illustration of this phenomenon.[5] If someone accidentally disclosed to his close brothers in Christ that he was cheating on his wife, they would immediately become deeply alarmed and confront him with his sin. They would most likely also quickly involve their priest in an effort to address this problem. However, if someone else openly and even boastfully told these same brothers that he had just spent a huge financial windfall on a variety of self-indulgent luxuries, it is highly unlikely that they would confront him with his covetousness. Indeed, they would probably congratulate him on his "success." Most likely their priest would never be called on to get involved.

God, however, sternly warns us about the extreme dangers of both sexual sin and covetousness. The author of Hebrews mentions God's judgment on both: "Marriage should be honored by all . . . for God will judge the adulterer and all the sexually immoral. Keep your lives free from the love of money [i.e., covetousness]" (Heb 13.4–5 NIV). Paul says that both of these sins will exclude people from the kingdom of God: "For this you know, that no fornicator . . . nor covetous man . . . has any inheritance in the kingdom of Christ and God" (Eph 5.5). Cortines and Baumer emphasize the seriousness of both these sins: "It's easy for us to agree that unrepentant, flagrant

[5]Generous Giving, *Alan Barnhart–God Owns Our Business*, June 30, 2014, video, 16:58, *https://vimeo.com/99540117/*, accessed September 2, 2021.

sexual sin indicates a lack of true faith or devotion to Jesus. But the Bible says the same is true for unrepentant, flagrant coveting. . . . *Spending all of our income on ourselves in the pursuit of fulfillment, to the detriment of our generosity, is like regularly committing adultery.*"[6]

We may draw an analogy between the funding problems of our organizations and a person with a severe headache. Doctors in a hospital emergency department can temporarily relieve the pain of a headache with morphine. But if they neglect to identify and treat the underlying illness causing the headache, whether it be a tumor, stroke, or meningitis, the person may die. Our fundraising headaches are the result of the potentially spiritually fatal underlying illness of covetousness. But instead of treating this cause, we engage in periodic ministry-centric fundraising campaigns that are like injecting morphine. Sometimes the very chronicity of our fundraising difficulties and the urgency of our financial needs leads us to believe that we need to adopt the same kinds of periodic fundraising efforts, capital campaigns, and development departments that the worldly nonprofits around us use. Rarely, if at all, do we engage in any serious spiritual reflection regarding whether these fundraising approaches that we have imported are even Christian—that is, whether they are faithful to the Scriptures and the patristic tradition. We often entirely ignore the fact that these organizations that we emulate have entirely ministry-centric financial goals that lack any concern for the souls of their donors. Often these fundraising strategies seriously undermine and even oppose God's efforts to heal covetous idolatry. From a long-term perspective, therefore, they do far more harm than good. They are like injecting arsenic rather than morphine.

It is perfectly legitimate for church organizations to present information about programs that need funding as well as exciting visions for future projects. But such appeals should always be presented within the context of a loving soul-centric approach that emphasizes why giving would be helpful for the salvation of the

---

[6]Cortines and Baumer, *True Riches*, 35 and 37. Emphasis in the original.

person to whom we are speaking, not how much good our organization could do with the donation. The "ask" should always be a prophetic call for the hearers to deepen their experience of the love of God in their own hearts. Such spiritual growth is the only kind of inducement to give we should ever offer. We should seek to avoid worldly inducements such as matching gift programs, elegant banquets featuring prominent bishops or Orthodox celebrities, "silent auctions," placing red ribbons around the necks of donors, and public donation acknowledgments in written materials or on plaques on donor walls. While such programs do have the patina of promoting godly generosity—and they occasionally do raise significant amounts of money—in the long run they dangerously subvert the Christian spirituality of our people. The common denominator of all these inducements—indeed, the reason they work so well in the world—is their appeal to the pride of donors. They therefore serve as supercharged fertilizer for the thornbushes that choke out the fruitfulness of the seed in the third soil. If, instead of using such fundraising techniques, we strove to nourish the growth of the seed in the fourth soil, the resultant thirty, sixty, and hundredfold spiritual and financial growth would far outstrip our ability to contain it. The financial results from such an approach may take far less time than we fear and be far more successful than we could possibly have expected.

Fr Joseph Corrigan's discipline of faithful financial teaching discussed in the last chapter has already demonstrated the success of such an approach in a parish context. This parish with one hundred members, at least one third of whom were children, regularly had an income of about $300,000. And one year it exceeded $500,000. It should be emphasized that this was not a parish in a wealthy Beverly Hills community. The vast majority of the people lived within a few blocks of one another in an area affectionately called "The Patch." This was in a lower-middle-class neighborhood in Pomona, one of the poorest cities in California, located a few miles from the parish temple, which was in the city of San Dimas. Parishioners gave generously to the parish and regularly experienced the bless-ings of doing so. Even more significantly, many of the children of the parish have continued to experience the blessings of tithing and generosity as they have entered their own work lives and had their own families.

Paul's highly effective soul-centric fundraising project in behalf of the poor in Jerusalem provides another model for a godly fund-raising approach. He alludes to this project in several of his letters, but describes it at greatest length in chapters 8 and 9 of 2 Corin-thians.

He begins chapter 8 by referring to his recent fundraising success among the churches of Macedonia. The truly remarkable thing about that work was that he concentrated his efforts among poor people. This is because his fundraising goal was not primarily raising money but saving souls. Such a soul-centric effort is not a priority for most of our fundraising programs. These programs typically emphasize appeals to people with "financial capacity." Even Christian develop-ment officers who often see themselves as having a sacred vocation to nurture spiritual growth and generosity in the lives of the faith-ful must prioritize their efforts among wealthier people. Although Christians of low or modest income need to learn about generosity just as much as wealthy people do, they simply don't have enough potential donation dollars to even cover the salaries of the develop-ment department. It should therefore be obvious that, despite their godly intentions, the most important priority of most development departments is to raise money. Promoting spiritual growth is neces-sarily only a secondary goal.

Paul, however, was not constrained by such concerns. So he taught about generosity even to poor people. His soul-centric mes-sage was so successful that despite their poverty the Macedonians "urgently pleaded with [Paul] for the privilege of sharing in this service to the Lord's people" (2 Cor 8.4 NIV). Paul then explains that what prompted this eagerness to give financially was that "they gave themselves first of all to the Lord" (2 Cor 8.5 NIV). Then, even though they were poor, they spontaneously "gave as much as they were able, and even beyond their ability" (2 Cor 8.3 NIV). In other words, Paul first ministered to their hearts, curing their covetousness, and then their donations joyfully followed.

We aren't told what Paul said to the Macedonians, but presumably it was similar to what he wrote to the Corinthians. A list of several of these things is shown below. What may be most striking to us about this list is what is completely absent from it. Paul never mentioned the worthiness of the cause to which he was asking them to give nor how desperately their contributions were needed. This is entirely contrary to the advice of worldly fundraising consultants who often urge us to emphasize the tremendous good that donations will accomplish. If he had wanted to, a man of Paul's eloquence could have easily described the suffering of the undernourished children and mothers in Jerusalem with emotionally irresistible pathos. But he didn't. Instead, Paul saw the needs of the poor in Jerusalem that prompted his entire fundraising effort as a providential opportunity for the Corinthians to grow spiritually and to glorify God. He did this by presenting at least nine soul-centric reasons for why they should give. Three of them explicitly state that God would bless them for their generosity.

1. He stirs up the gratitude of the Corinthians for the great sacrifices that Jesus has already made in their behalf. "For you know the grace of our Lord Jesus Christ, that though he was rich, yet for your sakes he became poor, so that you through his poverty might become rich" (2 Cor 8.9 NIV).

2. He encourages them to concentrate on the act of giving itself, not the amount. "For if the willingness is there, the gift is acceptable according to what one has, not according to what one does not have" (2 Cor 8.12 NIV).

3. Their giving would demonstrate the mutuality of their love for their distressed brethren in Jerusalem. This is the oneness that Christ said would make manifest the fact that the Father

had sent Jesus into the world (Jn 17.20–23). In addition, they could be confident that, if they ever had financial difficulties, their efforts at achieving oneness would be reciprocated. "Our desire is not that others might be relieved while you are hard pressed, but that there might be equality. At the present time your plenty will supply what they need, so that in turn their plenty will supply what you need. The goal is equality" (2 Cor 8.13–14 NIV).

4. He says that God will bless them for their generosity. "Remember this: Whoever sows sparingly will also reap sparingly, and whoever sows generously will also reap generously" (2 Cor 9.6 NIV).

5. Their giving is a matter of their personal relationship with God. "Each of you should give what you have decided in your heart to give, not reluctantly or under compulsion, for God loves a cheerful giver" (2 Cor 9.7 NIV).

6. A second time he promises God's blessing on their giving. "And God is able to bless you abundantly, so that in all things at all times, having all that you need, you will abound in every good work. As it is written: 'They have freely scattered their gifts to the poor; their righteousness endures forever'" (2 Cor 9.8–9 NIV).

7. A third time he says that God will bless their giving. "Now he who supplies seed to the sower and bread for food will also supply and increase your store of seed and will enlarge the harvest of your righteousness. You will be enriched in every way so that you can be generous on every occasion" (2 Cor 9.10–11 NIV).

8. Because of their generosity, great thanksgiving will pour out to God. "And through us your generosity will result in thanksgiving to God. This service that you perform is not only supplying the needs of the Lord's people but is also

overflowing in many expressions of thanks to God" (2 Cor 9.11–12 NIV).

9. The recipients of their gifts will pray for them. "And in their prayers for you their hearts will go out to you, because of the surpassing grace God has given you" (2 Cor 9.14 NIV).

Hudson Taylor adopted a fundraising approach that epitomizes a God-pleasing organizational approach to this issue. He was a well-known Protestant missionary in the 1800s who spent several decades in China attempting to proclaim the Christian gospel in a culturally sensitive way. His efforts were the foundation of much of the explosive growth of the Christian faith currently taking place in China despite the severe persecution that Christians in that country now endure. He and the many hundreds of missionaries with whom he worked made it a policy never to solicit donations from anyone for their own needs or for the sake of their ministry. Instead they committed all their financial needs to God in prayer. As a result of this fundraising approach, this large number of people living in a foreign land and in a strange culture never lacked adequate provision. Hudson Taylor's faith has subsequently had a powerful effect on many prominent Protestants, including the evangelist Billy Graham and Olympic gold medalist and missionary Eric Liddell, whose story was told in the movie *Chariots of Fire*.

When some people questioned Hudson Taylor about the wisdom of his decision never to ask for donations, he replied, "The Lord is faithful. . . . People say, 'Lord, increase our faith'. . . . It is not great faith you need . . . but faith in a great God. . . . Let us see to it that we keep God before our eyes; that we walk in His ways, and seek to please and glorify Him in everything, great and small." He then summarized his entire perspective: "Depend upon it, God's work, done in God's way, will never lack God's supplies."[7]

[7]Howard Taylor, *Hudson Taylor and the China Inland Mission: The Growth of a Work of God* (London: Morgan & Scott; Philadelphia: China Inland Mission, 1919), 428–429.

Mother Teresa took the same approach to fundraising that Hudson Taylor did. In her book *The Soul of Money*, Lynne Twist writes, "When I visited [Mother Teresa] at her orphanage in India, I asked her if she had any advice about fund-raising. She replied that her method of fund-raising was to pray, and that God had always provided what she needed, never more, never less. She operated with no reserves, trusting that God would always provide, and in her experience God always did. She operated more than 400 centers in 102 countries, and they always seemed to have exactly what they needed."[8]

An approach that would reorient our fundraising efforts toward the gospel's soul-centric emphasis would be for organizations to accept donations only from people who fulfill two specific conditions. The first would be that they must have already given their ten percent offering to their local parish. Such a condition would love potential donors by encouraging them to experience God's blessing on tithing. It would likewise love our parishes by demonstrating a strong commitment to directly support them while also minimizing any potential competition for donor dollars. If parishes consequently have far more money available to give away, then the fundraising demands on Christian ministry leaders would be vastly simplified. They could simply discuss their financial needs with priests and parish councils. The whole current unhealthy church fundraising infrastructure would simply evaporate.

The second condition would be that, in addition to already tithing to their parish, potential donors must not have any outstanding consumer debt. If they do, organizations seeking donations should ask them to spend whatever money they were thinking about giving to the organization on retiring their debt. The love for potential donors that this exhibits is obvious.

It would, of course, be inappropriate to rudely interrogate potential donors about their personal finances. However, it would be easy

[8]Lynne Twist, *The Soul of Money: Transforming Your Relationship with Money and Life* (New York: W.W. Norton and Company, 2017), 103–4.

to clearly state both giving conditions in all fundraising brochures and presentations.

Some people believe that fundraising efforts that focus on building spiritually meaningful relationships with potential donors can be a powerful means for encouraging generosity and thereby assisting donors on their spiritual journey. They also believe that encouraging people to spend their money on their ministry passions will help them lead more fulfilling lives. In some cases, both these goals might be worthwhile. Nevertheless, the test of our integrity in doing this will be clearly shown by the frequency with which we try to accomplish these goals with poor people as often as we do with the wealthy. The ministry-centric fundraising efforts of worldly nonprofits that concentrate their efforts among rich people often successfully provide substantial charitable assistance to the poor, local hospitals, and schools, and even funding for research to cure various diseases. Such projects are worthy of our respect and help make the world a better place. The goal of Christian fundraising, however, is not primarily to raise the money required to make this world a better place but to emulate God's soul-centric concern for the spiritual prosperity of our people. It is to build disciples who glorify God: "My Father is glorified by this, that you bear much fruit, and so prove to be my disciples" (Jn 15.8 NASB). Paradoxically, intensely concentrating on building disciples rather than raising money, especially striving to heal the covetous idolatry that lurks in all our hearts, will ultimately raise far more money than even the most effective worldly fundraising techniques.

The Scriptures consistently teach that the most important thing any of us can do as individuals to seek God's spiritual and financial blessing is to live faithful Christian lives. David wrote of the man who lives righteously, "He shall be like a tree planted by the rivers of water, that brings forth its fruit in its season, whose leaf also shall not wither; and whatever he does shall prosper" (Ps 1.3). The same principle applies to Christian organizations. Both our spiritual and financial success depend on striving with all our hearts to do God's work in God's way, as Hudson Taylor said. Fundamentally, all truly Christian fundraising is simply the incarnation of the soul-centric teaching of Jesus regarding how to live without financial worries: "Seek first the kingdom of God and his righteousness, and all these things shall be added to you" (Mt 6.33).

If, however, we find that we lack enough faith to trust God for the success of this approach, we still have hope. First, we should straightforwardly and honestly acknowledge this weakness to ourselves, God, and one another. The resultant humility may itself powerfully attract God's grace, and cause him to meet our financial needs. Second, even if our lack of faith compels us to occasionally use ministry-centric fundraising methods, we should not abandon the quest for more godliness in our efforts. St John Chrysostom's Easter Sermon beautifully describes God's kindness and compassion toward those who, despite their weakness, strive to do better: "For the Master is gracious and receives the last, even as the first; he gives rest to him that comes at the eleventh hour, just as to him who has labored from the first. He has mercy upon the last and cares for the first; to the one he gives, and to the other he is gracious. He both honors the work and praises the intention."[9] May our infinitely generous and merciful God bless even our present ministry-centric fundraising efforts according to the sincerity of our good intentions to gradually increase our practice of soul-centric efforts in the future.

Questions for reflection

1. Why is covetousness more than a "victimless sin" that only affects the spiritual life of the covetous person?

2. Why do wealthy people in the church give less than poor parishioners on a percentage basis?

[9]John Chrysostom, *Paschal Homily*. In *The Services of Great and Holy Week and Pascha*, 746.

3. What do you think about the following statement: "From a long-term perspective, therefore, [worldly fundraising techniques] do far more harm than good. They are like injecting arsenic rather than morphine"?

4. How can we discover if we have covetous idolatry in our hearts, and how much of it there is?

5. Why do we talk far more in our parishes about sexual sin than covetousness when, as has been discussed previously, God talks far more about money than sexual sin?

6. What do you think about the following statement: "Depend upon it, God's work, done in God's way, will never lack God's supplies"? Suppose that the consequence of living according to such faith is that our ministry or parish faces the threat of closure. Why might that be a good thing?

7. What would be the spiritual and financial consequences if our parishes and Orthodox institutions implemented Paul's soul-centric fundraising approach and stopped using techniques such as matching gift programs, celebrity banquets, and the like?

8. What would be the spiritual and financial consequences if our Orthodox organizations adopted the two giving conditions mentioned above (i.e., only accepting donations from people who have already tithed and who have no consumer debt)?

9

A Parish Christian Financial Paradigm

An essential prerequisite for parishes to successfully teach about almsgiving is that they must first align their own financial priorities with those of the kingdom of God. One of the major reasons many serious Christians do not presently tithe to their local parishes is that they are troubled by how their parishes spend money. One particular story illustrates this issue.[1] There is a man in one of our parishes who for many years had been a Protestant pastor. In this role he not only consistently tithed himself but also regularly taught his entire congregation to do so. As the result of many years of prayer and study, he became convinced of the truth of the Orthodox tradition, and of his need to join it. He therefore gladly sacrificed his satisfying pastoral ministry in order to become an Orthodox layman and took up a secular job. For his first few years in Orthodoxy he continued his usual practice of tithing to his church. However, he then became frustrated at his parish's financial priorities. Instead of caring for poor people, even fellow parishioners with significant needs, the parish financially prioritized acquiring new icons and saving money in order to one day build a beautiful new temple. He ultimately felt morally compelled to stop tithing to his parish and to give elsewhere.

Beautiful churches, theological purity, historical *bona fides*, and liturgical rigor are worthless "sounding brass and clanging cymbals" if they are not accompanied by practical expressions of love.

[1]The subject of this story has kindly allowed the author to share it, and remains anonymous by request.

Prioritizing such expressions would be especially important with the newfound financial abundance that parishes might receive by adopting the kind of teaching message advocated in previous chapters of this book. Before considering what those loving acts might be, it would be healthy for parishes to first embrace a spirit of financial contentment. God provides to each parish, just as to each of us as individuals, precisely the amount of money he wants us to have. If this is not enough for what the parish wants, then perhaps these wants exceed God's will. If a parish lacks enough money to meet basic expenses, then perhaps God wants major changes to take place in the way the parish functions. Perhaps it is a sign that the priest needs to pay more attention to the spiritual impact of misguided financial priorities among his people. If the local faithful are not sufficiently committed to giving tithes and offerings, then maybe God wants the parish to close. Facing the urgency of such a situation might be precisely the means God uses to spur parishioners to experience the blessings of godly generosity. If the people of a parish are too poor to support the needs of the parish, then this might be a glorious opportunity for a neighboring financially well-off parish to help them. This would be a modern-day reenactment of the apostle Paul's own ministry of mercy as he carried gifts from distant churches to help the poor in the church in Jerusalem. It would also provide a powerful demonstration of the unity of the Body of Christ.

Parish financial priorities will always proclaim what we believe about God far more clearly than our words, both to those within our parish and to outsiders who observe us. As we consider what these priorities should be, one of the issues that often arises is the budgetary importance of projects such as buying icons, otherwise beautifying our temples, and even new temple construction. As we ponder the wisdom of such projects, we need to remember that throughout the Scriptures God's overwhelming financial priority is care for the poor.

The centrality of this concern is powerfully stated by Isaiah and in several homilies of St John Chrysostom. Isaiah 58 addresses a complaint from the people of God that he does not seem to be answering their prayers:

> "Shout it aloud, do not hold back.
>> Raise your voice like a trumpet.
> Declare to my people their rebellion
>> and to the descendants of Jacob their sins.
> For day after day they seek me out;
>> they seem eager to know my ways,
> as if they were a nation that does what is right
>> and has not forsaken the commands of its God.
> They ask me for just decisions
>> and seem eager for God to come near them.
> 'Why have we fasted,' they say,
>> 'and you have not seen it?
> Why have we humbled ourselves,
>> and you have not noticed?'
> . . . .
> "Is not this the kind of fasting I have chosen:
> to loose the chains of injustice
>> and untie the cords of the yoke,
> to set the oppressed free
>> and break every yoke?
> Is it not to share your food with the hungry
>> and to provide the poor wanderer with shelter—
> when you see the naked, to clothe them,
>> and not to turn away from your own flesh and blood?
> Then your light will break forth like the dawn,
>> and your healing will quickly appear;
> then your righteousness will go before you,
>> and the glory of the LORD will be your rear guard.
> Then you will call, and the LORD will answer;
>> you will cry for help, and he will say: Here am I."
>> > (Is 58.1–3, 6–9 NIV)

Aesthetically beautiful temples and liturgical worship are extremely important. They lift our spirits to the heavenly realms and often draw people to the healing presence of Christ. Russia became Orthodox because of the awe-inspiring beauty of the worship at Hagia Sophia in Constantinople. Professor Timothy Patitsas' recent book, *The Ethics of Beauty*, provides a deeply moving and refreshing reflection on why attending to beauty is so important for bringing meaning and even healing to many areas of life, especially its traumas. Our culture particularly needs beauty because of our default tendency to see the pursuit of Truth as primarily an intellectual or philosophical endeavor. He underlines the importance of beauty for the spiritual life by pointing out that "the central text about Orthodox Christian prayer life, *The Philokalia*, itself means 'the love of the beautiful.'"[2]

It is, therefore, extremely important that we heavily invest in bringing as much beauty to our churches as possible. There are, however, different kinds of beauty, some more important than others. The beauty of icons, vestments, Gospel covers, and church domes is awe-inspiring, but there is nothing in the whole universe that quite matches the beauty of a human soul that manifests the love of God. In the fiftieth of his *Homilies on the Gospel of Matthew*, St John Chrysostom says that the beauty God most strongly longs for us to display in our churches is not that of "golden vessels, but of golden souls."[3] These "golden souls" can't be found in the catalogues of liturgical supply houses. They are acquired by generous acts of mercy by our people and parishes toward poor people. Regarding beautifying temples, Chrysostom says, "And these things I say, not forbidding munificence in these matters [that is, referring to adorning the temple] but admonishing you to do those other works [such as caring for the poor] together with these, or rather even before these. Because for not having done these no one was ever blamed, but for those, hell is threatened, and unquenchable fire, and the

---

[2]Timothy G. Patitsas, *The Ethics of Beauty* (Maysville, MO: St. Nicholas Press, 2019), iv.

[3]John Chrysostom, *Homilies on the Gospel of Matthew* 50.4 (NPNF[1] 10:313).

punishment with evil spirits. Do not therefore while adorning His house overlook your brother in distress, for he is more properly a temple than the other."[4]

In the twentieth of his *Homilies on Second Corinthians*, Chrysostom says that it is entirely good and proper to reverence the beautiful altar in a parish temple because it receives the Body and Blood of Christ during the Liturgy. But in close proximity to our parish we may find altars worthy of even greater reverence. Mother Teresa said that these altars are far more than blessed furniture; they are Jesus himself "in the distressing disguise of the poor."[5] Chrysostom says, "But you honor indeed this [stone] altar, because it receives Christ's body; but him that is himself the body of Christ you treat contemptuously, and when perishing, you neglect him. This [latter] altar may you everywhere see lying, both in lanes and in market places, and may sacrifice upon it every hour; for on this too is sacrifice performed. And as the priest stands invoking the Spirit [by the epiclesis], so do you too invoke the Spirit, not by speech, but by deeds [of love for the poor]."[6]

One of the signs that it is time for a parish to build a beautiful new temple, or even to provide beautiful adornments, will be the provision by God of more than adequate funds. Each of the three worship structures built in the Old Testament had immediately available extravagant financial support. The first was the tabernacle in the wilderness. It has already been pointed out that the overwhelming gratitude of the people for Moses' intercession in their behalf produced an abundant outpouring of donations that far exceeded the capacity of the workmen to receive them. The second Old Testament worship structure, the temple built in Jerusalem by King Solomon, also had abundant resources readily available for its construction. God had blessed King David with vast amounts of

[4] John Chrysostom, *Homilies on the Gospel of Matthew* 50.5 (NPNF[1] 10:313). Minor stylistic changes made to update the language for modern audiences.

[5] Becky Benenate, *In the Heart of the World* (Novato, CA: New World Library, 1997), loc. 183, Kindle.

[6] John Chrysostom, *Homilies on Second Corinthians* 20.3 (NPNF[1] 12:374). Minor stylistic changes made to update the language for modern audiences.

wealth, which allowed him to make a huge donation to this project. His generosity inspired many others to also give generously. But perhaps the clearest example of the role of God's providential provision for temple construction is the postexilic temple built in the fifth century BC. The money required to construct this temple apparently came almost entirely from a foreign leader who was not even a member of the people of God: Cyrus, King of Persia. Ezra recorded the details: "Now in the first year of Cyrus king of Persia, that the word of the LORD by the mouth of Jeremiah might be fulfilled, the LORD stirred up the spirit of Cyrus king of Persia, so that he made a proclamation throughout all his kingdom, and also put it in writing, saying, 'Thus says Cyrus king of Persia: All the kingdoms of the earth the LORD God of heaven has given me. And he has commanded me to build him a house at Jerusalem which is in Judah'" (Ezra 1.1–2).

We even have one New Testament example of a worship structure funded by someone who was not a member of the people of God. A Roman centurion who wanted Jesus to heal his severely ill servant was too humble to present his request in person. The Jewish elders he asked to go in his behalf told Jesus that this centurion was worthy of having his entreaty answered because "he loves our nation, and has built us a synagogue" (Lk 7.5).

One example of a way to prioritize the use of parish funds is as follows: (1) Give a tithe of all parish income to the diocese or archdiocese as a statement of faith in God's provision (see Num 18.26, Neh 10.38). (2) Financially support the priest and provide for adequate facilities. (3) Set aside money in an emergency fund. (4) Assist people in our own communities, such as the needy poor, retired priests, the elderly, and even our young people, who may need help with educational expenses. (5) Fund local or national Orthodox schools, colleges, seminaries, and missionary organizations. (6) Help needy poor people who live geographically close to the parish, as well as those in distant parts of the world. (7) New temple construction as confirmed by God's providential provision of the funds to do this.

Establishing such financial priorities not only aligns parish priorities with the financial priorities of God but models godly financial management to our own people. For example, setting the tithe as the first line item in every parish budget will encourage everyone in the parish to do the same in their personal budgets.

An additional aspect of parish finances worth exploring concerns how to understand and apply Jesus' teaching at the end of Matthew 6 in which he commands his disciples not to be anxious about money. "Look at the birds of the air," he says, "they do not sow or reap or store away in barns, and yet your heavenly Father feeds them. Are you not much more valuable than they? . . . And why do you worry about clothes? See how the flowers of the field grow. They do not labor or spin. Yet I tell you that not even Solomon in all his splendor was dressed like one of these" (Mt 6.26, 28–29 NIV). Citing these examples, he then says to us, "So do not worry, saying, 'What shall we eat?' or 'What shall we drink?' or 'What shall we wear?' For the pagans run after all these things, and your heavenly Father knows that you need them. But seek first his kingdom and his righteousness, and all these things will be given to you as well" (Mt 6.31–33).

Believing such a promise of God's provision to each of us as individuals requires a personal degree of faith that few Christians have. Suppose, however, that this promise is not made to each of us as individuals, but to our church communities as a whole. This would mean taking seriously the words of Paul: "For as we have many members in one body, but all the members do not have the same function, so we, being many, are one body in Christ, and individually members of one another" (Rom 12.4–5). He then goes on to list some of the gifts that are essential for the healthy functioning of any parish community, such as prophecy, teaching, serving, and leading. Two of the gifts he mentions are relevant to God's promise of financial provision in Matthew 6: "Having then gifts differing according to the grace that is given to us, let us use them: . . . he who gives, with liberality . . . he who shows mercy, with cheerfulness" (Rom 12.6, 8).

Orthodox Christians often exchange the greetings "Christ is in our midst" and "He is and ever shall be." The exercise of God's providential gift of wealth by those who have received it for the sake of the poorer brethren in our own parishes would perhaps proclaim to the world around us that Christ truly is in our midst more powerfully than the most powerful of sermons or the most persuasive historical accounts of apostolic succession and the consistency of our sacramental tradition. "Bear one another's burdens," Paul said, "and so fulfill the law of Christ" (Gal 6.2). Christians in the church of Acts provided an example of the evangelistic power of such a witness. It is said of them: "All who believed were together, and had all things in common, and sold their possessions and goods, and divided them among all, as anyone had need." As a fruit of this manifestation of the life of God in their midst, "the Lord added to the church daily those who were being saved" (Acts 2.44–45, 47).

The Church often describes herself as a family. We call the priest "father," the Church "mother," and fellow parishioners "brothers and sisters" in Christ. We have godparents and godchildren. Even Jesus used familial terminology for his followers: "Pointing to his disciples, he said, 'Here are my mother and my brothers. For whoever does the will of my Father in heaven is my brother and sister and mother'" (Mt 12.49–50 NIV). Paul clearly teaches that our first financial priority should be our own household (1 Tim 5.8). But once household needs are adequately met, then perhaps we might consider giving flesh and bones to the frequent statements that our fellow believers are indeed family. If any of us had a biological parent, sibling, or child who had significant financial needs, most of us would gladly help them. The same should apply to our spiritual relatives. Surely, if there is any place where we should apply God's second great commandment to love our neighbor, it is within the family of our own parish community. Everyone, of course, is entirely free to choose not to meet the personal and financial needs of brothers and sisters or even fathers in Christ. In this case, however, perhaps personal integrity demands that we should also adopt non-familial terminology to describe these relationships.

If we lack the faith to engage in mutual support on the grand scale that the church of Acts did, we can at least start doing this in small ways. Fr Jon Braun, a retired priest from St Athanasius Antiochian Orthodox Church in Santa Barbara, once described how his parish did this. The parish leadership strongly encouraged all its members to tithe for the sake of their own spiritual blessing. For those members who faced unexpected financial difficulties and therefore could not afford to tithe despite striving hard to live financially responsible lives, the parish would often provide them financial assistance with essential expenses such as rent and utilities so that they could tithe. The parish fully expected that in short order God's blessing or his leading to change their circumstances would enable these people to improve their financial situations and tithe on their own. The church also helped its members in other ways. Fr Jon described one situation in which a faithful parishioner with a wife and several children had a job that paid him substantially less than he needed to adequately cover his monthly expenses. He couldn't afford the gap in income that would occur if he left his current job in order to look for another. But he also feared that asking his boss for a raise might get him fired. He faced an impossible dilemma. After considering his situation, the parish leaders advised him to ask for a raise with the promise that if he got fired the church would cover his expenses until he found a new job. When this man proceeded to ask for a raise, his employer gushed about what a great job he was doing and promptly gave him a substantial increase in pay.

On one occasion Moses discussed the importance of mutual generosity within the community of the people of God. The law of Israel required that every seventh year creditors must forgive all debts. A potential issue might therefore arise if a poor person needed a loan and it was already the fifth or sixth year of the seven-year cycle. Quite understandably, many people were, therefore, reluctant to give a loan during these years because there was probably not enough time for the borrower to repay it before it had to be forgiven. If this happened, the loan would become a total loss. Moses sternly warned that such a way of thinking would anger God. He encouraged the people to give generously despite this risk because regardless of whether they were repaid, God would greatly bless them:

> If anyone is poor among your fellow Israelites in any of the towns of the land the LORD your God is giving you, do not be hardhearted or tightfisted toward them. Rather, be openhanded and freely lend them whatever they need. Be careful not to harbor this wicked thought: "The seventh year, the year for canceling debts, is near," so that you do not show ill will toward the needy among your fellow Israelites and give them nothing. They may then appeal to the LORD against you, and you will be found guilty of sin. Give generously to them and do so without a grudging heart; then because of this the LORD your God will bless you in all your work and in everything you put your hand to. There will always be poor people in the land. Therefore I command you to be openhanded toward your fellow Israelites who are poor and needy in your land. (Deut 15.7–11 NIV)

One of the most fascinating parts of this passage is the following statement: "There will always be poor people in the land." It almost seems as if God is saying that he will ensure the constant availability of people who need our financial help. This parallels the comment mentioned earlier, attributed to Chrysostom, that "the poor exist for the salvation of the rich." It is extremely important to note that these needy poor people were not strangers on the other side of the world. They were "poor people in the land . . . your fellow Israelites." The poor people in our own parish community, our own needy "brothers and sisters" and "fathers and mothers" in Christ, are not potential financial burdens to those with money. They are God's loving provision for the sake of our own blessing. They will enable us to experience the wonderful result that Moses promised: "God will bless you in all your work and in everything you put your hand to."

Questions for reflection

1. What do you think about the following statement: "Parish financial priorities will always proclaim what we believe about God far more clearly than our words, both to those within our parish and to outsiders who observe us"? What message do our current parish priorities proclaim? What message do we want to proclaim?

2. What do you think about the following statement: "The beauty God most strongly longs for us to display in our churches is not that of 'golden vessels, but of golden souls'"?

3. What do you think about the following statement: "One of the signs that it is time for a parish to build a beautiful new temple, or even to provide beautiful adornments, will be the provision by God of more than adequate funds"?

4. Should well-off parishes help poor parishes or their priests who struggle with severe financial difficulties? Why or why not?

5. What would it look like if all the members of our parishes used their money as if everyone were truly brothers and sisters in Christ, just as in our biological families?

6. Is there a need in your parish that might be addressed by accepting God's challenge in Isaiah 58, quoted above? How might you put this into practice?

7. What do you think about helping people in our parishes with tithing or with other financial difficulties? How would we ensure that they are being financially responsible with the money they are being given? If they are unwise about

debt issues, should we help educate them? How does Moses' comment, "There will always be poor people in the land," affect such decisions? How should we view the possibility that some people might abuse our generosity?

10

Almsgiving by Poor People

Jesus sat down opposite the place where the offerings were put and watched the crowd putting their money into the temple treasury. Many rich people threw in large amounts. But a poor widow came and put in two very small copper coins, worth only a few cents. Calling his disciples to him, Jesus said, "Truly I tell you, this poor widow has put more into the treasury than all the others. They all gave out of their wealth; but she, out of her poverty, put in everything—all she had to live on." (Mk 12.41–44 NIV)

I n addition to the simple facts given in this brief story, there are some inferences that we can easily draw about this woman's life and deed that we should consider. We don't know this lady's name, so we will call her "our widow" in this discussion. First of all, to state the obvious, at some point she had been married, and then her husband had died. Because of her poverty, she almost certainly had no living children. In her culture, children had the responsibility to financially support poor parents, especially a mother. At that time children were what we today call IRAs, 401(k) plans, and Social Security. This explains why one of Jesus' most important last concerns while hanging on the cross was to ask the Apostle John to care for his mother. Mary was already a widow and was soon to become childless.

We don't know our widow's age. Possibly she was an old woman who had lived many years with her husband but couldn't have children, suffering the ignominy of barrenness, like Joachim and Anna.

Perhaps she did have children, but they had died, causing her that most painful of maternal griefs, burying one's own child. It is also possible that she was young and had suffered the heartbreak of being tragically widowed shortly after her wedding, not having been married long enough even to have children. Whatever the case was, she had undoubtedly experienced tremendous suffering in her life. We can also infer that she must have been terribly alone. If her parents had been alive, or if she had siblings or good friends, surely they would have tried to alleviate some of her severe poverty. It is obvious, of course, that given her destitution she was poorly clothed and often hungry, eating as little and infrequently as possible in order to conserve her dwindling financial resources. In the midst of so much suffering she deeply understood the words of the psalms: "Darkness is my closest friend" (Ps 88.18 NIV).

We first meet our widow a few days before Passover, on Tuesday of Holy Week. At the time of this story, it was the sacred duty of all Jews to make the long journey to Jerusalem every year to celebrate the feast of Passover, as the Gospels record Jesus himself regularly doing. So perhaps a few months before Passover she had started to consider whether she should go to the feast this year. Undoubtedly the trip would involve at least some additional expense that she could ill afford. But despite the obvious financial imprudence, something deep inside her heart impelled her onward to see if just possibly she had enough money for the trip. Indeed, she did, but just barely. By the time she arrived in Jerusalem, all she had left were two small coins.

Part of one's spiritual responsibility in coming to the Passover feast was to bring a gift to God (see Tob 1.6–8). Our widow knew this, but what was she to give? If she gave even one of her two small coins, how could she buy the bread she needed to live even a few more days? "Furthermore," she thought, "is there really any point in me giving such a small amount of money to the temple? What the temple needs is big donations, from rich people. My two small coins aren't going to make the slightest dent in the temple budget." She agonized in prayer trying hard to discern the will of God concerning this matter. Alas, she heard nothing from him. Finally, she decided, "If it is the final thing I do in my life, let me spend these last two small coins on the love of God."

So, on Tuesday she entered the temple grounds, heading for the donation box. In its vicinity stood several clusters of people, many of them quite rich, who had just made large donations to the temple. They were rejoicing with one another about how deeply grateful they felt for God's abundant blessing on their lives, which had enabled them to give so generously both to the work of the temple and to the needs of the community. Our widow, frail from near starvation and wearing tattered clothes, slowly weaved her way quite inconspicuously through this small crowd until she finally arrived at the donation box. For a moment she just stood there, feeling the power of life and death that the box held over her. In her hand she clutched the coins that were her lifeline to a few more days of bread. Beneath her hands loomed the opening in the box, a yawning chasm ready to swallow her last means of provision. After one last convulsion of indecision, she quietly prayed for God's mercy, unclenched her fist, and then heard the two coins land in the depths of the box with a soft thud. "Well," she thought, "the deed is done. My meaningless life full of misery and suffering is over. All I have to do now is find an unobtrusive place in which to quietly lie down and die."

But at that very moment, at the very instant when our widow released the coins from her clenched fist, something else happened that she could never have imagined possible. For at this precise moment the incarnate God and Creator of the universe, the Lord of lords and King of kings, the God of Abraham, Isaac, and Jacob, the God who had led her ancestors out of Egypt in the Passover, the Lord Jesus Christ was in the temple sitting near the donation box intensely watching her, and he saw what she did. His presence at that moment was not an accident but a divine appointment. God specifically came to meet her on this occasion because he had seen her many years of faithfulness in the midst of suffering and because he had heard her final prayers concerning her desire to give everything she had for the sake of the love of God. And he was apparently deeply moved by her offering.

Jesus used his presence at her offering to teach his disciples a very important lesson concerning how God measures offerings. Many worldly nonprofit organizations and our popular culture often seriously distort God's view of true generosity. They measure and honor the value of donations according to their financial magnitude. Furthermore, wealthy philanthropists often seek a degree of immortality by making large donations in order to have buildings or philanthropic programs named after them or their loved ones. Sometimes they have plaques placed in their honor. But God measures gifts not according to their financial magnitude but according to the sacrifice involved in giving them. The Gospel story of the widow records that, just prior to her donation, "many who were rich put in much" (Mk 12.41). Observing the enormous discrepancy between how much they gave and how much she gave, Jesus said, "Assuredly, I say to you that this poor widow has put in more than all those who have given to the treasury; for they all put in out of their abundance, but she out of her poverty put in all that she had" (Mk 12.43–44).

Because of God's view on the nature of true generosity, Jesus bestowed on our widow a degree of fame that even the wealthiest of philanthropists could never even dream of achieving. He ensured that her story was recorded in two of the four Gospels in the Bible—the bestselling book in the history of the world and the book that rests on the altar of every Orthodox church.

Paradoxically, poorer people often have a substantial advantage over wealthier people in obtaining the blessings of almsgiving. The $2,000 tithe of a waitress earning a poverty-level yearly income of $20,000 may involve far more personal sacrifice than the $500,000 parish donation of a business owner earning $1,000,000 a year. The waitress must seriously restrict her lifestyle in order to give this ten percent offering. However, even after his $500,000 gift the millionaire will still be able to live quite comfortably. Therefore, the offering of the waitress may be far more valuable than that of the wealthy man for the sake of attaining both the temporal and eternal rewards of almsgiving. Indeed, even a single dollar given by the waitress may represent more personal sacrifice in the eyes of God than the business owner's entire donation. Many of this world's most attractive financial investments are unavailable to those with little money. However, when it comes to the return on investment for mercy giving, poor people have a substantial investment advantage over the wealthy. Occasional sacrifices of small purchases that enable tiny gifts of mercy will, in turn, buy things of which the apostle Paul says, "Eye has not seen, nor ear heard, nor have entered into the heart of man the things which God has prepared for those who love him" (1 Cor 2.9).

Three further important observations should be made about our widow and her donation. First, our widow's fear that her offering would lead to starvation and death was badly mistaken. As soon as Jesus saw her utter poverty, and her generosity, he was undoubtedly deeply moved with compassion, as he had often been on many other similar occasions. As a result, he must have then instructed one or more of his disciples to do whatever was necessary to provide her with adequate food and clothing. Witnessing this active compassion on the part of Jesus may have been the occasion on which the apostle James first learned the principle about which he later wrote: "If a brother or sister is naked and destitute of daily food, and one of you says to them, 'Depart in peace, be warmed and filled,' but you do not give them the things which are needed for the body, what does it profit?" (Jas 2.15–16). Thus, the donation box that our widow thought was ready to swallow her up into death actually became the means God used to sustain her life.

Second, as has been pointed out, one of the reasons that our widow was so poor was because she had no children to support her. Alas, sadly, there was also another reason. Throughout the history of Israel, caring for the poor, especially widows and orphans, was one of God's highest priorities for his people. But the leaders of the temple had utterly failed her in this regard. The verses immediately preceding the story of our widow record Jesus saying, "Watch out for the teachers of the law. They like to walk around in flowing robes and be greeted with respect in the marketplaces, and have the most important seats in the synagogues and the places of honor at banquets. They devour widows' houses" (Mk 12.38–40 NIV). That they devoured widows' houses doesn't mean that they broke into their homes and stole their goods. These destitute widows had no homes worth breaking into nor any possessions worth taking. It means that the leaders of the temple did not obey God's commandments to provide for needy people like our widow.

Third, precisely because of this failure, our widow had an unassailable reason to be disappointed, even righteously angry, with the leaders of the temple who had behaved so disgracefully toward God and personally failed her so badly. But to whom did she give her offering? She gave it to this very temple. She gave because she understood that while it may superficially appear that her tithes and offerings were given to the temple, it was really God who received them.

That Tuesday was a banner day financially for the temple treasury because of the many large offerings given by many rich people. Spiritually, however, it ranks among the worst days in the history of the people of God. The enormous love for God shown by the generous offering of this insignificant widow strikingly contrasted with the failure of the temple leaders to love her. Therefore, her offering, the last offering recorded in the Scriptures under the old covenant, may have been the deed that sealed God's judgment on the spiritual bankruptcy of these leaders.

Our widow's life was full of hardship and poverty. But despite this she chose to continue giving generously to God. Because she faithfully gave not only a tithe but all she had, God exceptionally blessed and honored her. If we likewise remain faithful to God when adversity comes into our lives, as it inevitably will, by spending even a few of our small coins on the love of God, then we, too, may one day find ourselves recipients of a divine appointment and beneficiaries of God's generous compassionate provision.

Questions for reflection

1. Who is another poor widow whose story the Bible tells whom God blessed for her sacrificial giving? What lessons does her story teach about generosity?

2. What do you think about the following statement: "Paradoxically, poorer people often have a substantial advantage over wealthier people in obtaining the blessings of almsgiving. The $2,000 tithe of a waitress earning a poverty-level yearly income of $20,000 may involve far more personal sacrifice than the $500,000 parish donation of a business owner earning $1,000,000 a year"? What kinds of blessings might God bestow on the waitress that he might not be able to bestow on the businessman?

3. What would it look like if our churches and organizations consistently taught that God honors and blesses the magnitude of one's sacrifices rather than the amount of one's gifts? How would this affect our fundraising? In particular, how might it affect how we address those with wealth?

4. What is the most sacrificial gift, financial or non-financial, you have ever given? Are you glad you gave it, or do you regret it? Why? Did God reward your sacrifice? What are some of the other sacrificial gifts you have given? How did those turn out?

5. What do you think about the idea that we should continue giving to our parish even if we have the same kind of justification that our widow had to feel righteously angry about the behavior of the priest or the parish council?

6. Have you ever had an experience of God in a "divine appointment"? What were the circumstances?

11

Rewards for Almsgiving

Hundreds of passages in Scripture refer to God's blessing on righteous behavior. These include Malachi 3.10, Psalm 1, Psalm 111 (Psalm 112 in the Hebrew numbering), the fifth of the ten commandments (Deut 5.16), and even the Beatitudes in the Sermon on the Mount.

In order to bring more immediacy to this, it may be helpful to substitute the word "reward" for "blessing." Thus, instead of saying that God blesses tithing, we might say that he rewards tithing. Instead of saying that the merciful are blessed by subsequently receiving mercy (Mt 5.7), we might say that they will receive the future reward of mercy in return for the mercy they now show.

At first glance, the idea of seeking a reward from God for acts of loving generosity toward needy people or other acts of godly obedience may seem unspiritual or even boorish. It may offend our Christian sensibility that believes that all expressions of love for God and our neighbor should be disinterested, that true love never seeks anything in return for its efforts. It should be noted, however, that it is common for parents and schoolteachers to lovingly train their children and students with promises of reward or punishment. Apparently, this is also how God trains his children. Spiritual giants may not need such promises to encourage righteous behavior, but it appears that God thinks the rest of us do.

Indeed, the concept of seeking God's reward for righteous behavior is central to Christian faith. The distinction between an unbeliever and a Christian is not simply that the Christian believes that God exists. According to the apostle James, "even the demons believe" (Jas 2.19). The author of Hebrews says that the faith that pleases God not only "must believe that he is" but also that "he is a rewarder of those who diligently seek him" (Heb 11.6). Thus, true Christian faith involves far more than an intellectual assent to the existence of God. It even requires far more than regularly attending church and consistently practicing a variety of spiritual disciplines. The Pharisees did all these kinds of activities with extraordinary faithfulness. But Jesus completely disqualifies the faith of those who do such things without primarily seeking God's reward: "How can you believe, who receive honor from one another, and do not seek the honor that comes from the only God?" (Jn 5.44). Moses spoke at great length encouraging God's people to seek his rewards for righteous behavior: "Now it shall come to pass, if you diligently obey the voice of the LORD your God, to observe carefully all his commandments which I command you today, that the LORD your God will set you high above all nations of the earth. And all these blessings shall come upon you and overtake you, because you obey the voice of the LORD your God" (Deut 28.1–2). A long list of God's rewards for obedience then follows. Jesus repeatedly described God as one who rewards righteous behavior. When you do charitable deeds in secret, "your Father who sees in secret will himself reward you" (Mt 6.4). When you pray in secret, "your Father who sees in secret will reward you" (Mt 6.6). When you fast in secret, "your Father who sees in secret will reward you" (Mt 6.18). In the last chapter of the New Testament, Jesus gives one last great appeal for his people to seek God's reward: "And behold, I am coming quickly, and my reward is with me, to give to every one according to his work" (Rev 22.12).

Jesus himself, the perfect model for our own behavior, accomplished one of the most important acts of his life, dying on the cross in our behalf, for the sake of a reward. The reason Jesus "endured the cross, despising the shame," was "for the joy set before him" (Heb 12.2). The reward that his sacrificial death on the cross brought him, that he looked forward to with such joy, was the opportunity to make possible our salvation.

While God blesses obedience to all his commandments, there is an extraordinary number of commandments that specifically relate to his blessing on almsgiving. Often the promised rewards have nothing to do with finances, but involve God's blessing on all aspects of the generous person's life. Here is a small sampling of such scriptural promises:

1. If there is among you a poor man of your brethren ... you shall surely give to him, and your heart should not be grieved when you give to him, because for this thing the LORD your God will bless you in all your works and in all to which you put your hand. (Deut 15.7, 10)

2. I have been young, and now am old; yet I have not seen the righteous forsaken.... He is ever merciful, and lends; and his descendants are blessed. (Ps 37.25–26)

3. The generous soul will be made rich, and he who waters will also be watered himself. (Prov 11.25)

4. He who has pity on the poor lends to the LORD, and he will pay back what he has given. (Prov 19.17)

5. He who gives to the poor will not lack, but he who hides his eyes will have many curses. (Prov 28.27)

6. He who has a generous eye will be blessed. (Prov 22.9)

7. If you extend your soul to the hungry, and satisfy the afflicted soul, then your light shall dawn in the darkness, and your darkness shall be as the noonday. (Is 58.10)

8. Give, and it will be given to you: good measure, pressed down, shaken together, and running over will be put into your bosom. For with the same measure that you use, it will be measured back to you. (Lk 6.38)

Deeply steeped in such passages from the Scriptures, St John Chrysostom often proclaimed God's unfathomably great rewards for almsgiving. But on one occasion he even more powerfully emphasized the importance of giving alms by teaching that this discipline is vitally important not only for its own sake but for the success of all other ascetic efforts. It is almost as if he sees almsgiving as the keystone spiritual discipline for experiencing any of God's rewards for obedience.

In Jesus' parable of the ten virgins (Mt 25.1–13), five were foolish because they did not bring oil for their lamps and therefore could not enter the kingdom of heaven. The five wise virgins who did bring oil were able to enter. The Greek word for oil in this parable, *elaion*, sounds similar to the word for mercy, *eleos*, from which the word for almsgiving, *eleēmosynē*, is derived. St John deftly links the *elaion* in the virgins' lamps to the *eleos* demonstrated by almsgiving, as we shall discuss below. In order to understand the supreme regard that St John accorded almsgiving, we need first to appreciate how highly he, like many other great church fathers, esteemed the ascesis of virginity and monasticism. Fr Josiah Trenham described the reason for this high regard: "The presence of the Kingdom of Christ on the earth and in the heart of men can in no more drastic way be proved to the world than by observing the establishment of perpetual virginity and monastic life."[1]

In his discussion of this parable Chrysostom says of the five foolish virgins, "I am ashamed; I blush and weep when I hear that a virgin is foolish. After they had achieved so much virtue, trained in virginity, elevated their bodies to heaven and competed for superiority over the heavenly powers, I hear this statement [that five were foolish] and blush." He then comments on what made them foolish: "For virginity is the light, almsgiving the oil. Therefore, when the light does not have oil to burn safely and steadily, it is extinguished. Virginity is likewise extinguished when it lacks almsgiving."[2]

---

[1]Josiah B. Trenham, *Marriage and Virginity According to St. John Chrysostom*, 135–136.

[2]John Chrysostom, *On Repentance and Almsgiving*, trans. Gus George Christo,

Chrysostom then tells the foolish virgins how they should have bought oil:

> Who are the dealers of this oil? The poor, the ones who sit in front of the church in order to ask alms. How much do they sell it for? As much as you want. I do not put a price on it so that you may not qualify for poverty. Buy as much as you can. Do you have one obol?[3] Buy the sky. Not because the sky is cheap, but because the Lord is a lover of mankind. You do not even have one obol? Give a glass of refreshing water. *"The one who offers one glass of refreshing water to one of the least of these for my sake will not lose his reward"* [Mt 10.42]. Heaven is a business and an enterprise, and we are negligent. Give bread and seize paradise. Give small things and grasp great ones. Give mortal things and take firm hold of immortal ones. Give corruptible things and capture incorruptible ones.... Give to the poor, so that even if you keep silent (and thousands upon thousands of mouths defend you) almsgiving will take your side and plead on your behalf. Almsgiving is the salvation of the soul.... Have you washed your physical hands with water? Wash the hands of your soul with almsgiving. Do not use poverty as your excuse. The widow granted hospitality to Elijah during her worst state of poverty and poverty did not hinder her.... The foolish virgins did not enter into the bridal chamber, because they did not possess almsgiving along with virginity.[4]

At least three important observations can be made about these words of Chrysostom. First, Chrysostom vastly expands the purposes of almsgiving beyond the realm of simple human compassion. He says, "Heaven is a business and an enterprise." Far from portraying almsgiving as simply a purely disinterested expression of

---

[3][The *obol* was the coin of least value in the Roman Empire of Chrysostom's day.—*Ed.*]

[4]Ibid., 32–33, 36.

love, he portrays almsgiving as a very practical business investment opportunity that buys heavenly rewards. For those who might be bothered at such a transactional approach, it should be noted that Jesus also suggests a transactional connection between the right use of worldly wealth and heavenly benefits in his parable of the unjust steward: "Use worldly wealth to gain friends for yourselves, so that when it is gone, you will be welcomed into eternal dwellings" (Lk 16.9 NIV).

Second, Chrysostom describes God's exceeding generosity in transforming even our smallest gifts into astonishingly great spiritual rewards. "Do you have one obol? Buy the sky. . . . Give bread and seize paradise. Give small things and grasp great ones. Give mortal things and take firm hold of immortal ones." Who among us can resist such great returns for our investment in almsgiving?

The third observation is sobering. In the light of Chrysostom's beautiful portrait of God's infinitely great benevolence, his conclusion concerning the failure of the virgins to enter the kingdom of God is particularly damning: "The foolish virgins did not enter into the bridal chamber, because they did not possess almsgiving along with virginity." Without almsgiving our most sacrificial ascetic efforts are worthless. "For virginity is the light, almsgiving the oil."[5]

Diligently seeking God's rewards for our actions is not simply an optional activity for serious Christians; it speaks to the essence of whether we really do have God-pleasing faith. Since how we use our money is one of the clearest ways to manifest the true beliefs in our hearts (see Mt 6.21), tithing and almsgiving are among the most important spiritual disciplines we can ever undertake. The way Jesus talks about the five foolish virgins clearly demonstrates this. True love and faith should be uninterested only in earthly rewards.

[5]Ibid., 32.

Questions for reflection

1. What actions can we do that demonstrate our personal faith that God "is a rewarder of those who diligently seek him" (Heb 11.6)?

2. How does recognizing that God rewards obedience to his commandments affect your willingness to test God by tithing?

3. What do you think about the following statement by St John Chrysostom: "Heaven is a business and an enterprise"? How does this idea compare with Jesus' teaching in the parable of the unjust steward (Lk 16.1–13)? How does it affect your willingness to pursue an investment strategy that seeks to invest your "excess provision" not only for the sake of worldly profits but also for the sake of an eternal thirty, sixty, or hundredfold reward, as discussed in a previous chapter?

4. Is it fair that, after a lifetime of strict asceticism, any virgin or monastic should be excluded from the kingdom of God because they failed to give alms? Why or why not? To what other forms of asceticism besides virginity and monasticism might Chrysostom's comments about the need to add almsgiving apply?

5. Did any of the eight quotations from the Scriptures listed above that describe God's rewards for almsgiving appear particularly meaningful to you? Why?

6. How and where can we buy the kind of oil Jesus refers to in his parable of the ten virgins?

7. What do you think about the following statement: "Do you have one obol? Buy the sky.... Give bread and seize paradise. Give small things and grasp great ones. Give mortal things and take firm hold of immortal ones"? On what scriptural

basis does Chrysostom say that God offers such astonishingly great rewards for even small acts of almsgiving? What might God's generosity in our lives regarding such matters look like?

PART TWO

Non-financial Giving

12

Reconciliation

Therefore if you bring your gift to the altar, and there remember that your brother has something against you, leave your gift there before the altar, and go your way. First be reconciled to your brother, and then come and offer your gift. (Mt 5.23–24)

There are probably few circumstances that would cause any of our parishes, seminaries, or charitable organizations to tell us not to give a donation. Perhaps they might do so if they knew that the money we contemplated giving came from various kinds of criminal activities, such as the sale of illegal drugs or a Ponzi scheme that had defrauded our own parishioners. Even under these circumstances, some people might argue that it would be wrong to prevent someone from giving to God. Surprisingly, however, there is one circumstance in which God himself commands us not to give an offering. This is when, as referred to in the passage above, unresolved conflict exists between fellow disciples.

At first glance, the issue of mutual reconciliation may seem to be not only trivial but entirely irrelevant for the issue of giving to the church. But its importance becomes clear if we recognize that, in addition to money, Christians bring two other critically important gifts to the altar for the purpose of worship: our personal participation, and bread and wine.

First, we offer our active participation in the Liturgy. The word "liturgy," which we ultimately derive from the Greek word *leitourgia*, means "the work or public service of the people of God, which is the worship of the one true God."[1] Paul alluded to this work when he wrote to the Romans, "I beseech you therefore, brethren, by the mercies of God, that you present your bodies a living sacrifice, holy, acceptable to God, which is your reasonable service" (Rom 12.1). The second gift that we bring to the altar is the ordinary bread and wine that the Holy Spirit subsequently transforms into the Body and Blood of Christ. As we shall see, the issue of reconciliation is of such transcendent importance to Christian life that we should abstain from active participation in both the Liturgy and Holy Communion until we are reconciled and united in love with our fellow Christians.

Churches often place great emphasis on practices of personal piety, especially fasting, confession, and preparatory prayer, when discussing how we ought to prepare in order to commune worthily. In his commentary on the Gospel passage quoted at the beginning of this chapter, St John Chrysostom suggests that perhaps we ought to add reconciliation to this list. He writes, "This table receives not them that are at enmity with each other." Then, in order to ensure that we do not underestimate the importance of this issue, Chrysostom extends his admonition concerning the importance of reconciliation to even include prayer: "If it be but a prayer, which you are offering in such a frame of mind [i.e., a state of enmity], it would be better to leave your prayer, and become reconciled to your brother, and then to offer your prayer."[2] Paul also emphasizes the importance of reconciliation for Communion. The fundamental condition that made the Corinthians at risk of communing in an "unworthy manner" (1 Cor 11.27) was not lack of personal piety but their lack of reconciliation: "When you come together as a church, I hear that there are divisions among you" (1 Cor 11.18).

The early church treatise called the *Didache* provides what may seem to many of us an entirely unexpected explanation for why reconciliation is a matter of paramount importance for Commu-

---

[1] Glossary entry for "liturgy" in *The Orthodox Study Bible*, 1783.
[2] John Chrysostom, *Homilies on the Gospel of St. Matthew* 16.12 (NPNF[1] 10:112). Minor stylistic changes made to update the language for modern audiences.

nion:"" In accordance with the [commandment] of the Lord, gather together to break bread and give thanks, first confessing your failings, so that your sacrifice may be pure. Nobody who is in conflict with his companion should gather with you until they are reconciled so that your sacrifice is not defiled."[3] The *Didache* does not instruct unreconciled people to absent themselves from Holy Communion primarily for their own sakes. It admonishes them to stay away to avoid defiling the Holy Mysteries for everyone else. Near the beginning of his first letter to the Corinthians, Paul begs the Corinthian church to become united: "Now I plead with you, brethren, by the name of our Lord Jesus Christ, that you all speak the same thing, and that there be no divisions among you, but that you be perfectly joined together in the same mind and in the same judgment" (1 Cor 1.10). Perhaps Paul has this earlier injunction in mind when later in the letter he says, "Therefore whoever eats this bread or drinks this cup of the Lord in an unworthy manner will be guilty of the body and blood of the Lord. But let a man examine himself, and so let him eat of the bread and drink of the cup. For he who eats and drinks in an unworthy manner eats and drinks judgment to himself, not discerning the Lord's body. For this reason many are weak and sick among you, and many sleep" (1 Cor 11.27–30). Many Americans tend to interpret these words from an individualist standpoint. But in the context of the warnings of the *Didache*, perhaps the reason so many Corinthians were weak, sick, and dying was not that they themselves had neglected to fast before communing or otherwise to prepare themselves properly. Rather, perhaps, communing in a severe state of irreconciliation had seriously harmed all of them. The reason "he who eats and drinks in an unworthy manner eats and drinks judgment to himself" is because he causes so much harm to others in the church.

The danger of such irreconciliation arises because Communion mystically unites us not only with God but also with one another.

[3]*Didache* 14, translation in *On the Two Ways: Life or Death, Light or Darkness: Foundational Texts in the Tradition*, trans. Alistair Stewart(-Sykes), Popular Patristics Series 41 (Yonkers, NY: St Vladimir's Seminary Press, 2011), 42..

"Send down thy Holy Spirit upon us," the priest prays, "and upon these gifts here offered." Note that this prayer invokes God's presence both among the people and upon the bread and wine. Indeed, this invocation first mentions the people of God and then the Holy Mysteries. Scripture often emphasizes the extremely close connection between our relationship with God and our relationships with our brothers and sisters in Christ. For example, the Lord's Prayer teaches that God forgives us our sins "as we forgive those who trespass against us." Presumably, if we do not forgive others, God will not forgive us. Jesus' parable of the sheep and the goats in Matthew 25 shows that God completely identifies himself with the poor whom we either help or do not help. The Apostle John also clearly spoke of this linkage: "If someone says, 'I love God,' and hates his brother, he is a liar; for he who does not love his brother whom he has seen, how can he love God, whom he has not seen?" (1 Jn 4.20).

Many Orthodox Christians view preparation for Holy Communion as entirely a matter of personal piety, because they see theosis as a predominantly private ascetic struggle. Metropolitan Hilarion (Alfeyev) addresses this mistaken belief by saying of St Isaac the Syrian's personal ascetic pursuit, "This is the paradox of a solitary life; renouncing the world he does not cease praying for it. . . . Any thought of his own salvation apart from his brethren, was entirely alien to him."[4] John Romanides emphasized the same point: "The relationship of man with God should not be thought of as a man's own private matter. . . . In the New Testament, strictly individual relations with God alone do not exist, for Christians must also love one another exactly as Christ has loved them."[5] Over the centuries many saints have made enormous sacrifices in order to love other people. Some of them have even given up their own lives in order to save the life of another. As has already been mentioned, Moses loved his people so much that he even went beyond sacrificing his earthly

[4]Hilarion Alfeyev, *The Spiritual World of Isaac the Syrian*, Cistercian Studies Series 175 (Kalamazoo, MI: Cistercian Publications, 2000), 202.

[5]John S. Romanides, *The Ancestral Sin*, trans. George S. Gabriel, 2nd ed. (Ridgewood, NJ: Zephyr Publishing, 2005), 112–113.

life; he offered his eternal destiny in their behalf. Paul expressed his willingness to do the same: "For I could wish that I myself were accursed from Christ for my brethren, my countrymen according to the flesh" (Rom 9.3). Jesus made it clear that the goal of even the strictest ascetic fasting and prayer is not purification for its own sake but to grow in love. "By this all will know that you are my disciples," he said, "if you have love for one another" (Jn 13.35).

Part of the reason we pay so little attention to the importance of reconciliation for Communion is that it is a relatively rarely discussed topic among Orthodox Christians. Sermons and church retreats often address the topic of forgiveness. Many people, therefore, assume that reconciliation and forgiveness are the same thing. They are not. Forgiveness is a private and unilateral act of personal piety done entirely for the sake of one's own soul and personal relationship with God. This is why God asks us to forgive others regardless of whether they seek our forgiveness or not. Indeed, he calls us to forgive them even if they never acknowledge their sin against us and even if they forever remain unaware that they have wronged us. Jesus modeled precisely this kind of forgiveness from the cross: "Father, forgive them, for they do not know what they do" (Lk 23.34). Stephen did the same in the midst of his stoning: "Lord, do not charge them with this sin" (Acts 7.60).

In contrast, reconciliation is a relational process that no one can accomplish on their own. There is nothing private or unilateral about it. It strives to achieve the Trinitarian unity to which God calls the Church. Georges Florovsky wrote, "The Church is the likeness of the existence of the Holy Trinity, a likeness in which many become one."[6] Quoting one of the greatest Orthodox theologians, Dumitru Stăniloae wrote, "According to St Maximus the Confessor the purpose of the saints is 'to express the very unity of the Holy Trinity.'"[7] This is the unity Jesus asked for in his high priestly prayer:

[6]Georges Florovsky, *Bible, Church, Tradition: An Eastern Orthodox View* (Belmont, MA: Nordland, 1972), 44.

[7]Dumitru Stăniloae, *Theology and the Church*, trans. Robert Barringer (Crestwood, NY: St Vladimir's Seminary Press, 1980), 39.

I do not pray for these alone, but also for those who will believe in me through their word; that they all may be one, as you, Father, are in me, and I in you; that they also may be one in us, that the world may believe that you sent me. And the glory which you gave me I have given them, that they may be one just as we are one: I in them, and you in me; that they may be made perfect in unity. (Jn 17.20–23)

Often, confusion about the difference between forgiveness and reconciliation arises because of the assumption that asking for and receiving forgiveness from another person for our sin against him or her means that we are reconciled. In the case of trivial offenses, this may indeed be the case. Nothing further needs to be done because asking for forgiveness in this way is in itself an act of reconciliation. But in the case of more serious offenses—the kinds of sins that threaten significant relational breaches—much more than asking for forgiveness is required. Examples of such sins might include betrayals of community trust by church leaders, embarrassing another person in a public setting, false personal accusations, or betrayal of private confidences. In such situations, where serious offenses have occurred, simply asking for forgiveness may be a doorway for further reconciliation, but asking forgiveness by itself does not suffice to accomplish the reconciliation that we are called to pursue. If all we do is ask for forgiveness without more deeply seeking reconciliation, we risk severely devaluing the importance of our relationship with the other person. God wanted reconciliation with them enough to die for them, but we don't esteem them enough to seek to restore a healthy relationship. Seeking such relational unity will often involve a willingness to exercise the personal vulnerability required to uncover and openly acknowledge to the other person the reasons that lay behind our sin, such as pride or serious past wounds that we ourselves have suffered. Those who seriously seek to follow God will embrace such a process as an opportunity for personal spiritual growth and, even more importantly, to show godly honor and respect to the other person.

An illustration from marriage will help demonstrate the distinction between forgiveness and reconciliation. Marital disagreements occasionally arise because each spouse has brought to the relationship assumptions, often called "baggage," about the nature of family life. For example, one spouse may have grown up in a frugal family that expressed love through simple gifts and family outings such as camping or fishing trips. The other may have been raised by spendthrift parents who expressed love through expensive gifts and luxurious vacations. Neither spouse has sinned by internalizing either of these vastly different financial perspectives concerning how family members should give and receive love. No need exists to either seek or grant forgiveness. But it will require the process of reconciliation to address the collision of perspectives that will inevitably occur as this new family makes plans for celebrating holidays or other special occasions. Tight family finances may exacerbate the intensity of such conflicts. One spouse will worry about the cost of gifts. The other will worry about inadequately expressing love.

Actively striving to achieve reconciliation of this conflict will produce two extraordinarily valuable benefits. The means for accomplishing this will involve pursuing two overlapping processes. The first process is for each spouse to prayerfully and intensely consider his or her previously unexamined belief systems concerning how money should be used to express love in the light of the teachings of the gospel. Both husband and wife will thereby come to a much deeper biblical and patristic understanding of this issue than they ever had before. Synthesizing these new perspectives in the course of discussions with one another, perhaps with the help and guidance of a spiritual father, will then enable them to develop their own mutually agreed-upon, conciliar financial approach. The second process will overlap with the first. It involves the mutual self-disclosure and transparency that will occur as each spouse recalls how his or her own family of origin viewed both the topics of money and how to express love. Exploring such formative memories may often surface deeply painful memories. As these arise and are shared, each spouse will come to know the other better. Even more importantly, the love and comfort they will be able to provide one another regarding such past painful experiences will increase the depth of their emotional intimacy and trust. Thus, resolving the initial conflict through this process of reconciliation will lead to an extremely beautiful and valuable twofold benefit. Both spouses will have grown in their knowledge and application of the gospel and they will also have greatly strengthened their marital bond.

This same fruitful twofold benefit of reconciliation is available whenever conflicts arise in any close parish relationships. This is true regardless of the nature of the conflict or its subject matter. First, each person can explore his or her point of view concerning the issue at hand in the light of the gospel. Second, mutually vulnerable sharing and attentive listening to each other's point of view will allow the people involved the opportunity to significantly deepen their relational bonds. The more intense the conflict, the greater the potential relational growth. Regardless of whether such conflicts arise as a result of "baggage" or are a consequence of sin, the practice of reconciliation within our own parish walls is one of the most important gifts God offers the Church. It may also be a powerful contribution our churches can offer to help heal the apparently intractable serious polarization that is so prevalent in our surrounding culture.

Humility concerning our own sinfulness is a vitally important prerequisite for achieving reconciliation. The need for this is most acute when one person seeks to initiate the process of reconciliation by apologizing to another for a sin. Even when the matter is simple and forgiveness can easily be wholeheartedly granted, there is a danger that lingering awkwardness may persist in the relationship until genuine reconciliation has occurred. For at least some period of time, one person, the "magnanimous forgiver," may find himself relationally in a somewhat superior position to the "sinful supplicant." Such a relational inequity may particularly occur when a layperson seeks to begin reconciling with a clergyman by asking for his forgiveness. The person from whom forgiveness is sought may completely prevent this problem by quickly mentioning some of his own similar (or even worse) sins committed in the past. This allows both people to unite, to reconcile, as "sinful suppliants" at the one place where all true human unity and reconciliation most easily occurs: the foot of the cross.

Aleksandr Solzhenitsyn offers a perspective that can help us achieve the goal of becoming mutual "sinful suppliants." During his many years of terrible suffering in Josef Stalin's prison camps, he became aware of the sense of moral superiority that sometimes blinds people to their personal responsibility for seeking reconciliation, even when another person bears the primary responsibility for causing a conflict.

> It was granted me to carry away from my prison years on my bent back, which nearly broke beneath its load, this essential experience: how a human being becomes evil and how good.... And it was only when I lay there on rotting prison straw that I sensed within myself the first stirrings of good. Gradually it was disclosed to me that the line separating good and evil passes not through states, nor between classes, nor between political parties either—but right through every human heart—and through all human hearts. This line shifts. Inside us, it oscillates with the years. And even within hearts overwhelmed by evil, one small bridgehead of good is retained. And even in the best of all hearts, there remains . . . an unuprooted small corner of evil.[8]

By acknowledging these bridgeheads of both good and evil that exist in every human heart, as Solzhenitsyn mentions, we can easily make the choice to see ourselves in relationship to everyone else as a fellow "sinful suppliant." This is true whether the other person is our spouse, parent, fellow parishioner, coworker, a stranger, or even someone we otherwise despise for their evil behavior. When visiting prisoners in jail, we can explicitly identify ourselves to them

[8] Aleksandr Solzhenitsyn, *The Gulag Archipelago*, vol. 2, pt. 4, trans. Thomas P. Whitney (New York: Harper and Row, 1973), 615.

as fellow criminals under the law of God and mention the nature of our own offenses. When the temptation arises to judge church leaders, prominent politicians, or famous celebrities who make the news because of sinful or inappropriate actions, we can choose to immediately come alongside them by recognizing the evil that also lurks within our own hearts. When we learn about the large number of abortions performed in this country or of the evils perpetrated by powerful national or world leaders, we should feel enormous grief for the victims and a responsibility to right whatever wrongs are being done. But we can also recognize that our own ongoing sinfulness makes us complicit in these injustices at least to some degree.

When Paul told the Corinthians about the danger of communing in an "unworthy manner," he made an intriguing comment suggesting that God may even intentionally ordain the existence of such "factions." He said, "There must also be factions among you." He then proceeds to explain why such factions "must" exist. It is so "that those who are approved may be recognized among you" (1 Cor 11.19). The question then arises as to what it means to be "approved." It is often taught that this refers to people who maintain rigorously orthodox theological beliefs. However, while doctrinal purity and resisting heresy are certainly vitally important, possibly Paul here refers to something else in addition to dogmatic and canonical exactitude. Given the tremendous liturgical importance of reconciliation and Trinitarian unity, perhaps what Paul means is that "approved" leaders are those most capable of facilitating God-pleasing reconciliation and unity. The presence of "factions" makes it easy to identify who these leaders are. Any ordinary Christian leader can help righteous people live in peace and find salvation. But it takes a great leader, an "approved" leader, to help sinful people achieve reconciliation with God and one another. These are the leaders who most faithfully imitate Christ's own reconciling ministry that seeks to help the Church attain unity that imitates the unity of the Trinity.

The presence of conflicts not only reveals those who are truly "approved" church leaders but also those who are "approved" spouses, parents, in-laws, parish council members, teachers, work colleagues, and other kinds of leaders. For example, if one has a difficult relationship with a spouse or in-law, one can take the somewhat arrogant point of view that one deserves better than to be in a relationship with such a difficult person. Or one can take the view that whatever conflicts or "factions" that exist are ordained by God as opportunities for us to grow in spiritual maturity, so that we ourselves can be "approved" leaders who, like Christ, bring reconciliation. Perhaps we may even adopt the viewpoint that God blesses most those to whom he gives the greatest challenges, because in this way they will have the opportunity to imitate Christ most clearly.

Early portions of this chapter discussed the importance of having reconciled relationships as a prerequisite for healthy Communion. Without subtracting from the enormous importance of that truth, Fr Michael Gillis has provided some valuable reflections on how to apply it practically in our fallen world. Many people live with painful unreconciled relationships despite having tried everything within their power to achieve reconciliation. This may occur for a variety of different reasons. Sometimes the person with whom they hope to reconcile may be too personally insecure, proud, or even mentally ill to even attempt this process. When deep wounds have occurred as a result of serious offenses or abuse, it may take decades before sufficient healing allows a process of reconciliation to begin. Reconciliation may also be difficult to achieve because we ourselves lack the necessary relational skills required to make room for the other person to share their deepest feelings with us.

Thus, successful reconciliation may take a lifetime to achieve, or even await life in eternity. If we feel discouraged that we have unreconciled relationships, we can find hope by recalling that even two great pillars of the church, Paul and Barnabas, had a serious conflict but eventually reconciled. Barnabas insisted on taking John Mark with them on their missionary journey, while Paul strongly disagreed, and Paul and Barnabas parted ways (see Acts 15.36–40). In the epistles of Paul written after this event, however, we find friendly mentions by Paul of both Mark and Barnabas, indicating that this division was eventually overcome (see 1 Cor 9.6, Col 4.10, 2 Tim 4.11, and Philem 24).

Paul advises us on how to view any presently unreconciled relationships: "If it is possible, as much as depends on you, live peaceably with all men" (Rom 12.18). If we have attempted to fulfill Paul's counsel to do "as much as depends on [us]" then surely God's grace will fully cover any impediment that our irreconciliation might otherwise represent for the sake of our righteous participation in Holy Communion.[9]

When Jesus prayed for a sign to show the world that the Father had sent him, he did not ask for clergy who would heal the sick or raise the dead. He did not ask for beautiful chanting, icons, vestments, or temples. He did not even ask for churches that would feed and clothe the poor. While all these things are important, the primary thing he prayed for was our unity: "I do not pray for these alone, but also for those who will believe in me through their word; that they all may be one, as you, Father, are in me, and I in you; that they also may be one in us, that the world may believe that you sent me" (Jn 17.20–21).

Questions for reflection

1. What do you think about the distinction made above between forgiveness and reconciliation?

2. What experiences of attempted reconciliation have you had? Have some of these attempts gone well and others badly? What was the difference between these situations? If you have unreconciled relationships from the past, what are the barriers that now make achieving reconciliation difficult? How might you attempt to surmount these barriers?

---

[9]Author's personal communication with Fr Michael Gillis. As of the publication of this book, Fr Michael Gillis is the priest at Holy Nativity Antiochian Orthodox Church in Langley, British Columbia, Canada.

3. How can we encourage attempts at pursuing reconciliation to deal with conflicts in parish relationships?

4. What do you think about the idea of trying to always match someone else's apology to us with a statement describing similar (or worse) sins that we ourselves have done in the past? If you have not already tried this, would you be willing to consider doing this in the future as an experiment and then reflecting on why doing this may have been either easy or difficult to accomplish? If you have tried this, was there anything that made it difficult to do? How did it affect your relationship?

5. What do you think about the following statement by Aleksandr Solzhenitsyn: "The line separating good and evil passes not through states, nor between classes, nor between political parties either—but right through every human heart—and through all human hearts"?

6. What do you think about the description of an "approved" church leader as one adept at successfully reconciling even great sinners with one another and with God? How might an ordinary leader grow to become an "approved" leader?

7. What do you think about the following statement: "The presence of conflicts not only reveals those who are truly 'approved' church leaders but also those who are 'approved' spouses, parents, in-laws, parish council members, teachers, work colleagues, and other kinds of leaders"?

13

Treasure

Again, the kingdom of heaven is like treasure hidden in a field, which a man found and hid; and for joy over it he goes and sells all that he has and buys that field. Again, the kingdom of heaven is like a merchant seeking beautiful pearls, who, when he had found one pearl of great price, went and sold all that he had and bought it. (Mt 13.44–46)

The Gospel presentation of these parables emphasizes their importance in two ways. First, they are the fifth and sixth parables in a series of seven parables told in Matthew 13. Jesus told the first four to a "great multitude" standing around him on the shore of the Sea of Galilee. But he dismissed the crowd before telling these two parables. They were, therefore, a private instruction only for his closest disciples. Second, the way Jesus repeats similar ideas in quick succession is a typical Hebrew literary technique often used in the Scriptures to emphasize extremely important ideas, especially when God himself speaks.

At first glance, these parables appear daunting. They explicitly state that because the kingdom of heaven is so valuable, one must sell everything one possesses in order to acquire it. Such a demand creates a seemingly insurmountable barrier for anyone who has practical responsibilities in life, such as caring for a spouse, children, or elderly parents. Do these parables therefore implicitly require that everyone who seeks the kingdom must become a monastic?

The Scriptures frequently portray God as the one who takes the initiative in salvation. For example, through the burning bush in the wilderness, God called Moses to be his instrument to save his enslaved and suffering people in Egypt. "I have surely seen the oppression of my people who are in Egypt," God told Moses, "and have heard their cry because of their taskmasters, for I know their sorrows. So I have come down to deliver them out of the hand of the Egyptians" (Ex 3.7–8). God's desire for their salvation is a deeply personal matter. Before six of the ten plagues with which God subsequently confronted Pharaoh through Moses, God instructed Moses to tell Pharaoh, "Let *my* people go" (emphasis added). The ensuing Passover deliverance through the Red Sea has become the prototype of all of God's subsequent efforts to save *his* people. Through many of the prophets and the Psalms, God repeatedly proclaimed and demonstrated unrelenting love for his adulterous wife, Israel. Then, in the fullness of time, God again revealed himself and spoke through another "burning bush," the Theotokos. But this time, instead of sending an emissary like Moses to save his people, "God, who at various times and in various ways spoke in time past to the fathers by the prophets, has in these last days spoken to us by his Son" (Heb 1.1–2).

This brief recapitulation of salvation history clearly shows that the man in the two parables who sells everything in order to purchase the kingdom of heaven is Jesus. Selling everything, therefore, is not an impossibly difficult requirement that God imposes on us but a description of God's own efforts in our behalf. Jesus first sacrificed the wealth and glory of heaven for our sakes. As the apostle Paul says, Jesus, "being in the form of God, did not consider it robbery to be equal with God, but made himself of no reputation, taking the form of a bondservant" (Phil 2.6–7). He then sacrificed his life for our sake: "He who did not spare his own Son, but delivered him up for us all . . ." (Rom 8.32).

Thus, God treats us, his beloved creatures, as if we are the hidden treasure and pearl of great price that are worth his greatest sacrifice. As the apostle John wrote, it was "not that we loved God, but that he loved us and sent his Son to be the propitiation for our sins"

(1 Jn 4.10). Despite the wayward, adulterous, and contemptuous way we have treated him, God still deeply longs to bring us into his kingdom. God personified this unfathomably deep love through his command to the prophet Hosea: "Go again, love a woman who is loved by a lover and is committing adultery, just like the love of the LORD for the children of Israel, who look to other gods" (Hos 3.1). The author of Hebrews says of Jesus that it was "for the joy that was set before him [that he] endured the cross, despising the shame" (Heb 12.2). This joy set before him was the opportunity to restore his relationship with us, his adulterous spouse.

Having seen that Jesus is the one who sacrifices everything in behalf of us, we can now recognize the unfolding of a great mystery. It is that Jesus' own resurrection and exaltation from God occurred precisely as a result of this personal complete self-emptying effort to obey the Father in sacrificially loving us. Paul described what happened:

> ... Christ Jesus, who, being in the form of God, did not consider it robbery to be equal with God, but made himself of no reputation, taking the form of a bondservant, and coming in the likeness of men. And being found in appearance as a man, he humbled himself and became obedient to the point of death, even the death of the cross. Therefore God also has highly exalted him. (Phil 2.5–9)

According to Jesus, all who seek to find eternal life must pursue this same cruciform path: "If anyone desires to come after me, let him deny himself, and take up his cross, and follow me. For whoever desires to save his life will lose it, but whoever loses his life for my sake will find it" (Mt 16.24–25).

But while all Christians are called to this path, it is especially a calling to those who voluntarily accept positions as spiritual and financial leaders in the church: the clergy and the wealthy. This is because they serve as icons of Christ that all the rest of the faithful can strive to imitate. While we often recognize that members of the clergy are icons of Christ, wealthy people are also icons of Christ because the riches that God has providentially given them are God's intended means for fulfilling his frequent promises throughout the Scriptures to provide abundantly for his Church and the needy poor. They are icons because they tangibly model God's love, mercy, and generosity. The nature of their calling was explicitly proclaimed by Jesus to his apostles and to all subsequent church leaders: "You know that those who are considered rulers over the Gentiles lord it over them, and their great ones exercise authority over them. Yet it shall not be so among you; but whoever desires to become great among you shall be your servant. And whoever of you desires to be first shall be slave of all. For even the Son of Man did not come to be served, but to serve, and to give his life a ransom for many" (Mk 10.42–45).

As we strive to follow the cruciform path of Jesus, an instructive story about how one of our greatest saints, St Anthony the Great, started to do this provides us with an example of how we, too, can begin to enter this way:

> St Anthony had prayed to the Lord to be shown to whom he was equal. God had given him to understand that he had not yet reached the level of a certain cobbler in Alexandria. Anthony left the desert, went to the cobbler and asked him how he lived. His answer was that he gave a third of his income to the Church, another third to the poor, and kept the rest for himself. This did not seem a task out of the ordinary to Anthony who himself had given up all his possessions and lived in the desert in total poverty. So that was not where the other man's superiority lay. Anthony said to him, "It is the Lord who has sent me to see how you live." The humble tradesman, who venerated Anthony, then told him his soul's secret: "I do not do anything special. Only, as I work, I look at all the passers-by and say, "So that they may be saved, I, only I, will perish."[1]

---

[1]Gordon Mursell, *English Spirituality: From Earliest Times to 1700* (Louisville, KY: Westminster John Knox, 2001), 291–292.

When visitors subsequently asked St Anthony questions about who would be going to hell, he typically replied, "Hell is for me alone."

The cobbler's self-offering love in behalf of others is not unique to his own spiritual journey. It is the path of every spiritual and financial leader who wishes to lead and serve God's people faithfully. When praying for God to forgive the apostasy of his people, Moses said, "Yet now, if you will, forgive their sin—but if not, I pray, blot me out of your book which you have written" (Ex 32.32). To the Romans the apostle Paul wrote, "For I could wish that I myself were accursed from Christ for my brethren, my countrymen according to the flesh" (Rom 9.3). Many priests and other leaders in the history of the Church have imitated Moses and Paul in prayerfully offering their eternal destiny in behalf of other people. Even today there are leaders who do this. For example, Dr Frank Papatheofanis, the founder and president of the University of St Katherine, has often prayed since childhood in this way. These sacrifices offered in prayer, Jesus actually accomplished on the cross. First, he took on himself our sin: "For he made him who knew no sin to be sin for us, that we might become the righteousness of God in him" (1 Cor 5.21). Then he fully identified with us in our estrangement from God that sin causes: "My God, my God, why have you forsaken me?" (Mt 27.46). In the economy of God, the path to resurrection life only occurs through expressions of such sacrificial love.

Metropolitan Anthony (Bloom) of Sourozh told a story that describes the heart of clerical and financial leaders who wholeheartedly embrace the cruciform path of Jesus in their relationships with every other person in their lives, especially those that they may find difficult, challenging, and even adversarial:

> After the war [i.e., World War II] a document was found in one of the concentration camps. It was written on a torn sheet of wrapping paper by a man who died in this camp. And the substance of his message was a prayer in which he said, "Lord, when you come as a Judge of the earth, do not condemn the people

who have done such atrocious things to us; do not hold against them their cruelty and our suffering, their violence and our despair, but look at the fruits which we have borne in patience, in humility, in fortitude, in forgiveness, in loyalty, in solidarity; and may these fruits be accounted unto their salvation."[2]

This man's prayer follows the model that God the Father himself provided when "he made him who knew no sin to be sin for us, that we might become the righteousness of God in him" (2 Cor 5.21). It is one way to incarnate Jesus' command:

> Love your enemies, bless those who curse you, do good to those who hate you, and pray for those who spitefully use you and persecute you, that you may be sons of your Father in heaven; for he makes his sun rise on the evil and on the good, and sends rain on the just and on the unjust. For if you love those who love you, what reward have you? Do not even the tax collectors do the same? And if you greet your brethren only, what do you do more than others? Do not even the tax collectors do so? Therefore you shall be perfect, just as your Father in heaven is perfect. (Mt 5.44–48)

The story of Hannah Good (Channah Kopelowicz Gdud was her actual, non-Americanized name) provides another contemporary example of astonishing sacrificial love.[3] She was a brilliant

---

[2] Anthony (Bloom) of Sourozh, "The Raising of Jairus' Daughter," homily on November 18, 1984, *http://www.mitras.ru/eng/eng_143.htm*, accessed September 2, 2021.

[3] The author knows the remarkable story of Hannah Good from many personal conversations with her son William Good. "Uncle William," as my brother and I called him, was my father's best friend for over fifty years, and our families were close. He was one of the most amazing human beings many people have ever known. He had an exceptionally kind, generous, and gracious heart. He also had a brilliant mind, an impish sense of humor, and a gift for storytelling. He was a physician who was beloved by his patients. He continued practicing medicine in a poor Southern California community into his eighties, treating most of his patients without charge. In addition to this story about Hannah, there are many other stories that demonstrate astonishing personal goodness that the Gdud family participated in, both during the years of the Holocaust and subsequently. The *Los Angeles Times* ran two front-

woman widely recognized in her local community for her extraordinary kindness, generosity, and compassion toward all who were poor and needy. She had a reputation similar to that of the highly esteemed Tabitha concerning whom Luke wrote, "This woman was full of good works and charitable deeds which she did" (Acts 9.36).

Hannah and her husband, Dov, had two sons, William and Motl. The latter had a particularly sensitive disposition and was a musical prodigy with the violin. When the German blitzkrieg overwhelmed their hometown of Vilnius, Lithuania, in June 1941, Hannah and her family fled to a small town in the nearby countryside in order to escape the Nazi efforts to exterminate them because they were Jewish. At the time William was seventeen and Motl was fourteen. On the night of September 20, 1941, a friend in the town tipped them off to Nazi efforts to conscript the men of the town to dig graves in preparation for the imminent arrest and execution of all the local Jews. Hannah and Motl took refuge in a small hiding place that Dov had prepared in anticipation of just such an eventuality. Dov and William hid in the adjacent forest. After a difficult period of confinement, restless Motl decided to just briefly leave the hideout to look around. Unfortunately, local citizens promptly spotted him and hauled him off to the police station. When Hannah found out what had happened, she agonized over the terror that she knew gripped the heart and soul of her sensitive young son. She knew that he was now alone in a Nazi jail facing ruthless and brutal captors elated at the opportunity to snuff out his young life. The magnitude of the anguish of soul that gentle and kind Hannah must have endured in the midst of this crisis is unimaginable. She, her husband, and William gathered to discuss the situation. Together they grieved and lamented the tragedy that had befallen Motl. But then Hannah resolved that while she could do nothing to change his fate, she

page articles about William's life. The first was published on September 25, 2020. The second was published on December 26, 2020, the day after his death on Christmas Day. Both of these articles describe many details of William's life, but even more phenomenal stories of personal goodness and heroism are not included. William's wife, Pearl, and their three children, Lenny, Michael, and Hannah, are all remarkable people in their own right.

could do something to ease his suffering. She decided to voluntarily surrender herself at the police station, identifying herself as a Jew, so that she could accompany Motl on the final tragic journey of his life. Within days the Nazis mercilessly murdered Hannah and Motl with a hail of bullets launched from the depths of hell that was heard by Dov, William, and many others.

Theologians and philosophers could debate for years on end the wisdom of the decision Hannah Good had to make in the course of a few hours about whether to turn herself in to the police. From one point of view, she made a serious mistake by ignoring the sacred intrinsic value of her own life. In addition, she also deprived the world of much future goodness. Her exceptional intelligence, empathy, and generosity would undoubtedly have greatly blessed many needy people over the subsequent decades that she might have lived. She also had ongoing relationships with and responsibilities to her husband and elder son, both of whom deeply loved her. Other compelling arguments might also lead one to question the prudence of her decision. Against such eminently reasonable considerations one must weigh the astonished joy that undoubtedly overcame the distraught Motl when he saw his beloved mother "miraculously" materialize out of nowhere in the midst of his forlorn prison cell. Quite unexpectedly there she was hugging, comforting, and kissing him as she dissolved his terror, confusion, and despair in love. The pantheon of human compassion includes many heroes who have sacrificed their lives in exchange for the life of another person. One thinks of Maria Skobtsova, Maximilian Kolbe, and many others. They died so that others would live. However, unlike these other heroes, Hannah did not die in her son's place; she did not exchange her life for his. The most staggering feature of Hannah's sacrifice is that she made it entirely for the sake of simply comforting her terrified son for a brief time before his death. It has been said that on God's scale of justice and mercy even one small tear of repentance far outweighs great sins and leads him to grant forgiveness. The solution to the profound theological and philosophical debate over the wisdom of Hannah Good's choice may ultimately turn on how much frightened fourteen-year-old Motl's tears weighed on God's scale of compassion. Hannah obviously accorded those tears an almost infinite weight.

Her sacrifice may provide some people an insight into the relationship we have to those the Church honors as saints. It is often easy to see the icons of saints and to hear their stories in the synaxarion as representing a kind of ascetic "Hall of Fame." Contemplating their astonishingly difficult ascetic and martyric achievements may discourage those of us who know that such accomplishments far exceed our feeble ability to emulate them. This often makes it difficult to experience any kind of personal connection with the saints. Hannah's sacrifice, however, may open our eyes to see their holiness from an entirely different perspective. None of the saints pursued rigorous ascesis as an end in itself. They did it in order to more deeply experience God's love and to be able to express this love toward others, including us. The Church's seal on their sanctity confirms that they have grown so much into the likeness of God that whenever any of us might face an hour of great need or trial, or even an ordinary time of feeling lost or in pain, they would willingly offer as great a sacrifice of love in our behalf for the sake of as "small" a benefit as Hannah did for Motl. Reflecting on this may prompt us to develop increasingly tender connections with many saints, especially the Theotokos. It may also motivate us to strive more diligently than we ever have before in order to achieve the holiness that allows us to attain such greatness of relational love in behalf of those we know.

A story from the desert fathers helps explain the power of Hannah Good's story: "Abba Lot visited Abba Joseph and said to him, 'Abba, to the best of my ability I do my little *synaxis*, my little fasting; praying, meditating, and maintaining *hesychia*; and I purge my *logismoi* to the best of my ability. What else can I do?' The elder stood up and stretched out his hands to heaven; his fingers became like ten lamps of fire. He said to him: 'If you are willing, become altogether like fire.'"[4] In other words, we can strive to become "whole burnt offerings." Hannah Good's sacrificial act may have been a practical waste from a temporal standpoint, but, despite the fact that this had nothing to do with her intention, it may have allowed her to become in our eyes "all flame." The long-lasting and powerful influence of her deed on the lives of many people who have heard about it suggests that the most important legacy any of us could possibly leave our children and grandchildren is not a large financial inheritance but living our lives in such a way that we, too, become "all flame."

Three of the Gospels state that God's second great commandment is, "You shall love your neighbor as yourself" (Mk 12.31, Mt 22.39 NKJV; cf. Lk 10.27). This, of course, is a quotation from the law of Moses (see Lev 19.18). In the Gospel of John, Jesus explicitly expanded the meaning of this second commandment: "A new commandment I give to you, that you love one another; as I have loved you" (Jn 13.34). The addition "as I have loved you" clearly indicates that Jesus calls us to a standard higher than that of the Old Testament—we are now to love each other as Jesus himself has loved us.

In a personal letter to a friend, Pope John Paul II gave an insightful description of what this kind of love looks like: "After many experiences and a lot of thinking, I am convinced that the (objective) starting point of love is the realization that I am needed by another. The person who *objectively* needs me most is also, for me, *objectively*, the person I most need."[5] In other words, the most powerful experience of love that any of us can ever have is for another person to highly esteem the value of our love. Meeting the physical, emotional, or even spiritual needs of another person, even dying in that person's behalf, may represent an astonishingly noble act of agape love. But such deeds testify entirely to the greatness of the heart of the benefactor. The recipient of such love may remain an entirely impersonal

---

[4]Joseph of Panepho, Saying 7, translation in *Give me a Word: The Alphabetical Sayings of the Desert Fathers*, trans. John Wortley, Popular Patristics Series 52 (Yonkers, NY: St Vladimir's Seminary Press, 2014), 152.

[5]George Weigel, *Witness to Hope: The Biography of Pope John Paul II* (New York: HarperCollins, 2001), 102. Parentheses and italics in the original.

object of philanthropy. Seeking to love others as God has loved us means that we will seek intentionally, in every human relationship, to discover the blessing that the other person's life has for us. One of the most powerful ways we can do this is to strive to listen deeply to the life story and the heart of other people, no matter how severely disfigured by sin their lives may superficially appear to be. Such an investment in listening will almost always reveal some glorious element of value in the other person's life that may often greatly bless us. Meeting the needs of others proves the magnanimity of our souls. Discovering in what ways we can be blessed by their love affirms the greatness of their souls.

Often, other people need such an acknowledgement of their personal dignity almost as much as, if not more than, they need to have their physical needs met. This is not only true in the course of encounters between needy people and benefactors but in all our personal interactions, including those between husbands and wives, between parents and children, between pastors and their people, in the parish and at work, and even in the most casual encounters in daily life. The most powerful experience of love that any of us can ever have is for another person to esteem highly the value of our love for him or her. All of us need to be needed.

The complete helplessness of little babies demonstrates this phenomenon in a powerful way. Babies would die without the love of their mothers. This desperate neediness draws out of their mothers astonishing degrees of sacrificial love, even though babies have virtually no ability to reciprocate their love or express gratitude in return. Because of how desperately they are needed, mothers often experience in their relationship with their babies a degree of personal meaning and satisfaction that can scarcely be found in any other human interaction. For many mothers, the interminable sleepless nights and utterly exhausting days required to care for their little ones do nothing to detract from the affection that they feel for their babies. Often the magnitude of their affection continues to increase as their children need their mothers in different ways as they become toddlers, grade schoolers, and then adolescents. Indeed, the day her children leave behind an "empty nest"—that is, when her children leave home and no longer "need" her love—is often one of the most depressing days of a mother's life. Such is the power of the deep meaning that we experience when another person, even a helpless baby, desperately needs our love.

Clergymen also regularly have the experience of being deeply needed by other people. Their liturgical actions are required for parishioners to be able to receive the sacraments, including the Eucharist and confession, and to be able to pray other liturgical services. Parishioners also highly value them for the comfort they provide when their people face hardships, suffer the loss of loved ones, and need spiritual and practical wisdom for major decisions, as well as in countless other ways. Thus, despite the great personal hardships clergy often face, just as mothers do with their babies, being needed in these extremely important ways often provides them a wonderfully affirming sense of personal meaning. Several passages of Scripture implore parishioners to honor their priests for these sacrifices, both personally and financially: "Let the elders [Greek *presbyteroi*—that is, priests] who rule well be counted worthy of double honor, especially those who labor in the word and doctrine" (1 Tim 5.17). The Epistle to the Hebrews says, "Obey those who rule over you, and be submissive, for they watch out for your souls. . . . Let them do so with joy and not with grief" (Heb 13.17).

In addition to priests, Paul teaches that there are certain other people whom we should also greatly honor in our parish communities—those whom we would otherwise be most inclined to ignore. After emphasizing how the diverse members of the Church, the Body of Christ, are all essential, just as all the parts of the human body are needed for the well-being of the whole body, he then encourages us to honor the "less valuable" members of the body even more than we honor those with more prominent gifts: "Those members of the body which we think to be less honorable, on these we bestow greater honor" (1 Cor 12.23). Paul accentuates the importance and seriousness of this teaching by repeating the exact same point in the next verse: "But God composed the body, having given greater honor to that part which lacks it" (1 Cor 12.24). Note that Paul does not ask us to provide equal honor to all members of the Body of Christ: he asks us to bestow "greater honor" on those members whom we think to be "less honorable." This ought to be one of the most countercultural elements of church life.

Astonishingly, God himself models precisely this kind of love for each of us when we are weak, and even when we sin. The Old Testament repeatedly records God's laments when his people turn away from him and his longing for their return. One of the most powerful metaphors God used to convey the depth of his affection for us borrows from the relationship of helpless babies to their mothers that we have just discussed: "Can a woman forget her nursing child, and not have compassion on the son of her womb? Surely they may forget, yet I will not forget you. See, I have inscribed you on the palms of my hands" (Is 49.15–16). Jesus expressed the same kind of longing for the love of his people as he approached his death: "O Jerusalem, Jerusalem, the one who kills the prophets and stones those who are sent to her! How often I wanted to gather your children together, as a hen gathers her chicks under her wings, but you were not willing!" (Mt 23.37).

Mother Teresa's remarkable work that started in India and then spread around the world was not primarily inspired by a desire to obey God's commandment to love her neighbors. Rather, it arose out of a remarkable experience she had in which God opened her eyes to see the tremendous "thirst" he had for each one of us. Since intense thirst is one of the most powerful physical feelings that any person can have, the choice of this metaphor emphasizes the depth of this longing on God's part. As a result of her experience, Mother Teresa chose to devote her life to trying to express God's thirst to those whom many people would otherwise consider "less honorable" members of humanity: the poorest of the poor. She summarized the revelation that she received of God's thirst by writing a letter as if from God to each of us:

> It is true. I stand at the door of your heart, day and night. Even when you are not listening, even when you doubt it could be me, I am there. I await even the smallest sign of your response, even the slightest hint of invitation that will allow me to enter. . . .
>
> *I THIRST FOR YOU* . . . Yes, that is the only way to describe my love for you: I thirst to love you and to be loved by you. . . .
>
> *I thirst for you*—just as you are. . . . Have you not understood my cross? Then listen again to the words I spoke there, for they tell you clearly why I endured all this for you: "*I thirst*" (Jn 19:28). Yes, I thirst for you. . . .
>
> I stand at the door of your heart and knock. Open to me, for I thirst for you.[6]

Each of us is the "hidden treasure" and "pearl of great price" for which Jesus joyfully sold all that he had. The subtitle of this book, "The Good Way," therefore, uses the word "good" as an adjective to describe the inestimably great salvific value of almsgiving. And it also uses the word "Good" as a proper noun to honor the astonishing magnitude of the love that Hannah Good showed for Motl. Her story powerfully exemplifies God's own boundless love for each of us.

Questions for reflection

1. Did Hannah Good make the right choice to turn herself in? Why or why not? How important was her previous life of sacrificial goodness to her ability to decide to join Motl in prison?

---

[6]Joseph Langford, *Mother Teresa's Secret Fire* (Huntington, IN: Our Sunday Visitor Publishing Division, 2008), 297–300. Emphasis in the original.

2. What do you think about the following statement: "The most powerful experience of love that any of us can ever have is for another person to highly esteem the value of our love for him or her. All of us need to be needed"? In a parish meeting, at work, or even in your relationships with friends or coworkers, how important is it for you personally to know that your thoughts and presence are considered valuable? How does it feel when you feel that your presence is irrelevant?

3. What do you think about the following statement: "Meeting the needs of others proves the magnanimity of our souls. Discovering in what ways we can be blessed by their love affirms the greatness of their souls"? How can you do this? Who are some people who need your love? How does that make you feel?

4. How does considering the depth of the love of the holy saints for you personally rather than just their great ascetic achievements affect your veneration of them?

5. What lessons can we learn from the story of St Anthony's experience with the cobbler? How does it affect how we should think about the issue of who is going to hell and who isn't?

6. How does the astonishing prayer of the concentration camp victim affect how you view people in your life who treat you badly? How does it affect how you view your enemies?

7. How do you feel about praying in behalf of others in great need by offering up your salvation in their behalf? Could you do this with integrity? Why or why not?

8. How does it feel—and how does it affect your desire to pray—to realize that God thirsts for you?

9. What do you think about the following statement: "Note that Paul does not ask us to provide equal honor to all members of the Body of Christ: he asks us to bestow 'greater honor' on those members which we think to be 'less honorable'"? How do we live this out in our parishes?

Conclusion

Almost at the end of his life David offered a prayer that majestically conveys many of the ideas about money presented in this book. This prayer was uttered at the time when David and many others were offering vast amounts of money to build the Jerusalem Temple. It is worth noting David's comments about the gratitude to God that both prompted this offering and resulted from it.

Praise be to you, Lord, the God of our father Israel, from everlasting to everlasting. Yours, Lord, is the greatness and the power and the glory and the majesty and the splendor, for everything in heaven and earth is yours. Yours, Lord, is the kingdom; you are exalted as head over all. Wealth and honor come from you; you are the ruler of all things. In your hands are strength and power to exalt and give strength to all. Now, our God, we give you thanks, and praise your glorious name. But who am I, and who are my people, that we should be able to give as generously as this? Everything comes from you, and we have given you only what comes from your hand. We are foreigners and strangers in your sight, as were all our ancestors. Our days on earth are like a shadow, without hope. Lord our God, all this abundance that we have provided for building you a temple for your Holy Name comes from your hand, and all of it belongs to you. I know, my God, that you test the heart and are pleased with integrity. All these things I have given willingly and with honest intent. And now I have seen with joy how willingly your people who are here have given to you. Lord, the God of our fathers Abraham, Isaac and Israel, keep these

desires and thoughts in the hearts of your people forever, and
keep their hearts loyal to you. (1 Chr 29.10–18 NIV)

It is hoped that the discussion of money and salvation in this
book will encourage the leaders of parishes and Christian organizations to imitate the soul-centric approach of Jesus and Paul in all
financial discussions. It is also hoped that they will restore the spiritual pillar of almsgiving, including tithing, to its traditional place
of prominence alongside prayer and fasting in Orthodox life. This
would greatly assist all the faithful in their journey to experience
more deeply the love God has for us, both in this life and in eternity.
Far more importantly, it would help satisfy God's astonishingly great
longing for our salvation.

We know that God loves everyone. Only rarely do the Gospels single out a particular person as an object of this love. The rich
young ruler is one such person. Somewhat unexpectedly, Jesus did
not respond to this man's inquiry about how to inherit eternal life
by talking to him about his prayer, fasting, obedience, sexual purity,
or sacrificial love. Instead he took the risk of potentially seriously
offending him by talking to him about his money. Mark makes certain that we know that the reason Jesus did this was because he
"loved him" (Mk 10.21). Perhaps it is time for our leaders, especially
bishops and priests, to love our people in the same way. God may
respond to the obedience of such love and faith by pouring out on us
far more spiritual and financial fruit than we can possibly imagine.

Questions for reflection

1. If you are a clergyman, how do you feel about teaching your
   people about embracing a "Christian financial paradigm"
   in their personal finances, for example, concerning tithing?
   How could you make room for them to hear this message
   without thinking that your primary motive is merely ministry-centric—i.e., raising money for parish salaries, expenses,
   or infrastructure?

2. If you are a layperson, how do you feel about having more discussions in your parish about financial issues? How might you foster an atmosphere in which healthy discussions concerning financial issues could take place?

3. Note what David's prayer quoted above says about the providence of God regarding wealth and its transitory nature. How do these truths affect how you want to give to the church?

4. Why do you think the Gospel of Mark made it so abundantly clear that Jesus loved the rich young ruler? Who are the only other people that the Gospels specifically identify as people whom Jesus loved? (Hint: One of these is indirectly referenced several times, such as in John 13.23. Three others are mentioned in John 11.5.) Paul says that there is also a kind of person whom God loves. (Hint: See 2 Corinthians 9.7.) Why do you think God singled out these people in this way? Do they have anything in common?

Troparion (Tone 3)

From the wealth of your faith in God, thou didst distribute thy riches to the poor, O Philaret. Thy life was adorned with compassion and thou didst glorify the Giver of mercy. Implore him to have compassion and mercy on those who praise thee!

Kontakion (Tone 3)

Thou didst possess the spirit of Job in temptations, and compassionately distributed thy wealth to the poor. Thou wast a living fountain of almsgiving, and by thy manner of life thou didst gladden those who cry: Rejoice, O Philaret, servant of Christ God!

Icon by Kim Lukins (used with permission)

Praise for
Money and Salvation

ndy Geleris' *Money and Salvation* is much needed in our Ortho-dox Church as we encourage the faithful to be "like God." Andy emphasizes how generous and loving God is with specific biblical and patristic examples of giving as "soul-centric"—leading us to God—rather than "ministry-centric" regarding Church needs and projects. Everything we have is from God and is God's gift. The book also helps explain the great fruits and joy of understanding and living a life of generosity: the gift of an eternal life with God, beginning in our lives here and now.

Every parish council member and priest should read the book as they help their Church to thrive with a plan to help implement God's Kingdom. This involves not only providing the Church resources to do so but helping us, the faithful, to realize God's plan for drawing us closer to him in all aspects of our lives, putting our treasure and first-fruits in God's Kingdom rather than in the world. Our clergy and lay leaders can provide this example to the faithful by their own giving and a program of education, as the book suggests.

—Charles Ajalat

he Orthodox Christian teaching on salvation is based on the doctrine of free will. We make choices to be with God or to be without him. Everything that we do in Orthodoxy, be it Canon Law or Stewardship, is understood as a pathway given by God to attain salvation for those who choose it. In a rare read, Dr Geleris has illumined the path that shows us how we can use our earthly treasure in order to find salvation."

—The Very Rev Dr Chad Hatfield
President, St Vladimir's Orthodox Theological Seminary

Money and Salvation: The Good Way is not a book that will help you raise money. It is a book that will help you guide souls to salvation. Dr Geleris turns our thinking about money on its head and shows how Jesus and the Church Fathers taught that the Good Way of mercy opens the flood gates of heavenly mercy. It is a book that should be read by every priest and pastor and studied in parish book clubs, study groups, and adult Sunday schools.

—Rev. Michael Gillis
Pastor, Holy Nativity Antiochian Orthodox Church
(Langley, BC)

Dr Andrew Geleris has thought about, lived through, and discussed with me and others the substance of this book, which he has well organized on the theme of money in the Christian life. Andy's thesis is simple: Jesus taught us more on the theme of money and its associated passions and its possibilities than on any other theme. At first this claim is somewhat challenging to accept; yet Geleris' treatment of the biblical material in both the Old and New Testaments is deep, substantive, convincing, and pastorally significant. He distills the scriptural content thoroughly, offering even a specific paradigm for parochial priorities in financial management as a desirable product to guide churches in their life of ministry for Christ's sake. Patristic resources such as Chrysostom's priorities adorn the text throughout, for example, "Do not while adorning God's house overlook your brother in distress, for he is more properly a temple than the other." Geleris' treatment of the anonymous widow who cast in her last two mites is worth the price of the book all by itself. This reviewer is especially grateful for the author's emphasis on guiding people to retire their financial debt before considering themselves to be free (and thus, spiritually) financially. As I began this review so I end it: Dr Andy has experienced firsthand all that he writes about and lives it with great care (I dare say I've stolen some of his reward, God forgive!).

> — The Very Rev. Patrick B. O'Grady,
> Pastor, St Peter the Apostle Antiochian
> Orthodox Church (Pomona, CA)
> Assistant Professor of Liturgical Theology,
> Antiochian House of Studies (La Verne, CA)

This book is about sacrificial giving and salvation. It continues the spiritual guidance of St Basil and St John Chrysostom but adds a level of practicality that is often needed to apply such guidance. The author has derived an ethic of giving that is based on Old and New Testament writers who began the conversation. This foundation is expanded by later spiritual writers who have continued to emphasize the importance of generosity to the individual and the Kingdom. This is a much-needed book for the faithful who struggle with giving because they lack an understanding of its importance in spiritual life. It should be read and re-read and widely shared.

> —Frank Papatheofanis, M.D., Ph.D.
> Founder and President, University of Saint Katherine

As president of the Christian Research Institute, I read literally hundreds of books each year. *Money and Salvation* is among the most important and impactful. Dr Andrew Geleris rightly notes that while prayer and fasting are given their rightful due throughout the liturgical calendar, the Church has been remarkably remiss in proffering an adequate theology of money—this despite the reality that our Lord spoke more frequently and forcefully about almsgiving (mercy giving) than even about prayer and fasting. In this remarkable resource Dr Geleris balances the scales so that the cross hanging from the triple braided chain of almsgiving, prayer, and fasting drapes balanced around our necks as we progress toward eternity. This book is destined to create a major paradigm shift from loving money to loving God with all our heart and our neighbor as ourself. Read on. Be refreshed and renewed. I was!

—Hank Hanegraaff
Author of numerous books, including *Truth Matters, Life Matters More: The Unexpected Beauty of an Authentic Christian Life*

Dr Andy Geleris has taken an uncomfortable topic we would rather minimize and maximizes the salvific potential when we view money through eyes of mercy. *Money and Salvation* challenges our common approaches to church fundraising by returning to the biblical stories of sacrifice, whole burnt offerings, tithing, reconciliation, and mercy-giving. *Money and Salvation* has challenged me to reorient everything I value—my money, relationships, time, health, education, possessions, vocation, and faith—as gifts of God's great mercy. While I may be tempted to merely exchange these gifts in the marketplace, their value is realized—and perhaps even increased—when God's mercy provokes me to extend the same mercy I've been given. I encourage Christians to read this book with other Christians and to discuss the thoughtful questions at the end of each chapter. Studying its scriptural references will simultaneously enrich and inspire a merciful giver!

—Hollie Benton,
Executive Director of the
Orthodox Christian Leadership Initiative

Dr Geleris offers a heart-opening discussion that reminds each of us involved in ministry how important it is that we remember the journey in Christ we share with our neighbor. Our work should serve the soul and salvation of every person we touch each day—from the neighbor in need, to the volunteer, to the donor, to the person sitting next to us at a parish coffee hour. By mindfully keeping our ministries "soul-centric," we are better positioned to see the opportunities that the Lord presents for our community to grow stronger in Christ and, in turn, to build his Kingdom.

—Kenneth D. Kidd
FOCUS North America
(Fellowship of Orthodox Christians United to Serve)

So many of us in the Orthodox Church have wrongly understood the topic of money as taboo. Consequently, we teach and talk very little about it. Yet God has repeatedly revealed the importance he places on our correct thinking and handling of money. In his revolutionary new book, *Money and Salvation: The Good Way*, Dr Andy Geleris has refreshingly turned the contemporary Christian trends in thinking about money, talking about money, and using money, right-side up. By first revealing the spiritual importance God attaches to money and contrasting that with the insignificance many of us in Christendom attach to the subject, Andy has deftly highlighted the need to move from ministry-centric to soul-centric generosity—with humility, reconciled to others, and in a way that remembers it's all God's anyway.

With his usual graciousness and evident love for Christ and his Church, Andy walks us through the bold premise that the more you give, the more you have. Without mincing words, he gently invites his reader to consider a way of relating to money that looks nothing like the world tells us it should.

Money and Salvation is a must-read for anyone seeking to relate with money in a way that is glorifying to God. Part exegetical master class, part contemporary playbook, this frank and easy-to-understand guide is packed with critical insights, practical wisdom, and a deep study of the Orthodox Church's teaching on money in light of Holy Scripture and the writings of the Holy Fathers. In this noteworthy offering, Andy articulates the Church's wisdom in such a welcoming way that it just may transform the way you think about money now and forever. I cannot recommend it highly enough.

—Michelle Moujaes
Sustained Giving Team at Trinity Classical Academy
(Santa Clarita, CA)

D oes the use of money matter for salvation? Books on Orthodox spirituality typically avoid this question. While the lives of the saints contain the stories of those who renounced their wealth, a theology of money is lacking in Orthodoxy. Breaking the silence of the centuries, in his book *Money and Salvation*, Andrew Geleris provides a pioneering theological account of almsgiving. Taking the Old Testament concept of sacrifice as his starting point, the author offers a biblically grounded vision of almsgiving as a sacrifice of thanksgiving. Placing almsgiving in the context of the Eucharist, Geleris also discusses the practical aspects of tithing and the importance of financial literacy. Accessibly written and morally stirring, *Money and Salvation* will provoke a spiritual revolution in your parish, if its argument is taken to heart. Highly recommended!

—Paul L. Gavrilyuk, Ph.D.
Founding President of the International
Orthodox Theological Association

I strongly endorse this book. Dr Geleris has done an excellent job highlighting the importance of money in spiritual life. Although I now am involved in lay Orthodox Christian ministry, my professional career spanned four decades in the financial services industry on Wall Street. As a securities analyst, hedge fund manager, and the president of a large investment bank, my life's work revolved around money and the capital markets. Struggling with my own relationship with money, or leading people that were in a high-earning industry, created blessings and challenges of its own. This book does an outstanding job exploring the scriptural and patristic viewpoints on money and our relationship with it. Andy points out that we are called to focus on money's impact on our soul and salvation. This call is to us individually, as well as to the Church at large. This is a reorientation away from getting "stuff" done, to have money become part of our transformation process. I pray it bears much fruit for you as you read as it did for me.

—Paul P. Karos
Matrona Ministries, LLC

Orthodox Christian worship and the Orthodox Christian life experience involves sacrifice, and Orthodox Christian stewardship involves sacrificial giving. It is time we as Orthodox Christians move back to our roots on matters of money, parish finance, and personal financial practices. The early Church Fathers talked about the role of money and church finance but did so in the context of spiritual health, growth, and love; and the role that money plays in either impeding or enabling this health, growth, and love—all from an Orthodox Christian biblical understanding concerning money.

Through the centuries, however, Orthodox Christian financial practices moved in different directions around the world, and in North America they have moved to varied enterprising operations, like renting out the parish hall for banquets, catering, and weddings, as well as book stores, cultural food festivals, and even raffles, as the primary means to accomplish parish finance. Myriad reasons for this are discussed in this book.

These current practices that are used in North America for parish finance can be effective in funding the budget for the parish, except for one thing: they benefit the customers more than the parishioners. It is the customers that are giving money, at a good markup, and not the parishioners. And even if the parishioners are the customers, they are buying something in return for their giving, be it a meal, a dance, a good time, some cultural food, or a chance to win big. The one thing missing is the sacrificial giving of money by the parishioners. The whole Orthodox Christian life experience has a continual sacrificial practice at its core, and sacrificial giving, almsgiving, is very much a part of this practice, at least it was in the early centuries of the Kingdom, and we should bring it back into practice now.

The biblical teachings around the subject are illustrated beautifully in this book and provide a solid platform for an Orthodox Christian understanding of money, and its purpose, place, and value in the life experience of parishioners, as well as in parish finance. This book is indeed a valuable gift to the Orthodox Christian community.

—William D. Morrison

Chair of the Department of Stewardship, member of the Board of Trustees, and member of the Investment Committee of the Antiochian Orthodox Christian Archdiocese of North America